50 Walks in
SUSSEX &
SOUTH DOWNS

Produced by AA Publishing
© AA Media Limited 2013

First published 2001
Second edition 2008
New edition 2013

Published by AA Publishing (a trading name of AA Media Limited, whose registered office is Fanum House, Basing View, Basingstoke, Hampshire RG21 4EA; registered number 06112600)

Researched and written by Nick Channer
Field checked and updated 2013 by Tim Locke and Fiona Barltrop

Series Management: David Popey
Editor: Rebecca Needes
Designer: Tracey Butler
Proofreader: Donna Wood
Digital imaging & repro: Ian Little
Cartography provided by the Mapping Services Department of AA Publishing

Printed and bound in the UK by Butler, Tanner & Dennis

Mapping in this book is derived from the following products:
OS Landranger 186 (walks 32, 43, 44)
OS Landranger 188 (walk 21)
OS Landranger 189 (walks 1, 3, 4)
OS Landranger 197 (walks 30, 33, 34–42, 45, 47–50)
OS Landranger 198 (walks 18–20,22–29, 31, 35)
OS Landranger 199 (walks 2, 5–19)
OS Explorer 121 (walk 121)
Contains Ordnance Survey data © Crown copyright and database right 2013 Ordnance Survey. Licence number 100021153.

A05038

ISBN: 978-0-7495-7487-1
ISBN (SS): 978-0-7495-7513-7

The Automobile Association would like to thank the following photographers, companies and picture libraries for their assistance in the preparation of this book. Abbreviations for the picture credits are as follows: (t) top; (b) bottom; (l) left; (r) right; (AA) AA World Travel Library.

3 AA/D Forss; 8 AA/J Miller; 12/13 AA/J Miller; 24/25 AA/J Miller; 42 AA/D Forss; 49 AA/S & O Matthews; 70/71 AA/J Miller; 82/83 AA/J Miller; 90/91 AA/J Miller; 108 AA/P Brown; 113 AA/J Miller; 120/121 AA/L Noble; 148/149 AA/P Brown

Every effort has been made to trace the copyright holders, and we apologise in advance for any accidental errors. We would be happy to apply the corrections in the following edition of this publication.

The contents of this book are believed correct at the time of printing. Nevertheless, the publishers cannot be held responsible for any errors or omissions or for changes in the details given in this book or for the consequences of any reliance on the information it provides. This does not affect your statutory rights. We have tried to ensure accuracy in this book, but things do change and we would be grateful if readers would advise us of any inaccuracies they may encounter by emailing walks@theaa.com.

We have taken all reasonable steps to ensure that these walks are safe and achievable by walkers with a realistic level of fitness. However, all outdoor activities involve a degree of risk and the publishers accept no responsibility for any injuries caused to readers whilst following these walks. For more advice on walking safely see page 11. The mileage range shown on the front cover is for guidance only – some walks may be less than or exceed these distances.

Some of the walks may appear in other AA books and publications.

Visit AA Publishing at theAA.com/shop

Right: Pooh Bridge in Ashdown Forest (Walk 21)

50 Walks in
SUSSEX &
SOUTH DOWNS

50 Walks of 2–10 Miles

Contents

The Walks

Following the Walks

An information panel for each walk shows its relative difficulty, the distance and total amount of ascent. An indication of the gradients you will encounter is shown by the rating ▲▲▲ (no steep slopes) to ▲▲▲ (several very steep slopes). Each walk is rated for its relative difficulty compared to the other walks in this book. Walks marked +++ and colour-coded green are likely to be shorter and easier with little total ascent. Those marked with +++ and colour-coded orange are of intermediate difficulty. The hardest walks are marked +++ and colour-coded red.

MAPS

There are 40 maps, covering the 50 walks. Some walks have a suggested option in the same area. The information panel for these walks will tell you how much extra walking is involved. On short-cut suggestions the panel will tell you the total distance if you set out from the start of the main walk. Where an option returns to the same point on the main walk, just the distance of the loop is given. Where an option leaves the main walk at one point and returns to it at another, then the distance shown is for the whole walk. The minimum time suggested is for reasonably fit walkers and doesn't allow for stops. Each walk has a suggested map.

ROUTE MAP LEGEND

--▶--	Walk Route	▭	Built-up Area
❶	Route Waypoint	▭	Woodland Area
− − − −	Adjoining Path	🚻	Toilet
☀	Viewpoint	🅿	Car Park
•	Place of Interest	⊞	Picnic Area
⌂	Steep Section	)(	Bridge

START POINTS

The start of each walk is given as a six-figure grid reference prefixed by two letters indicating which 100km square of the National Grid it refers to. You'll find more information on grid references on most Ordnance Survey, AA Walking and Leisure Maps.

DOGS

We have tried to give dog owners useful advice about how dog friendly each walk is. Please respect other countryside users. Keep your dog under control, especially around livestock, and obey local bylaws and other dog control notices.

CAR PARKING

Many of the car parks suggested are public, but occasionally you may find you have to park on the roadside or in a lay-by. Please be considerate when you leave your car, ensuring that access roads or gates are not blocked and that other vehicles can pass safely.

WALKS LOCATOR

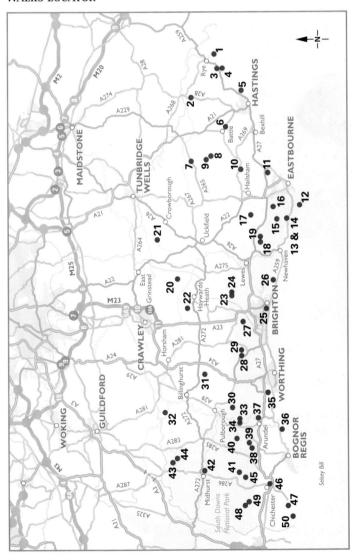

Walking in Sussex & South Downs

Divided into East and West Sussex back in 1888 for administrative purposes, Sussex is so typically English that to walk through its landscape will feel like a walk through the whole country. Within its boundaries lies a wide variety of landscape and coastal scenery, but it is the spacious and open South Downs with which Sussex is most closely associated.

This swathe of breezy downland represents some of the finest walking in southern England – an oasis of green in the midst of encroaching urban development. Designated an Area of Outstanding Natural Beauty and awarded full National Park status in 2011, the 90-mile (144km) chain of the Downs provide locals, as well as the many visitors, with a perfect natural playground. Kite flyers, model-aircraft enthusiasts, cyclists and hang-gliders are among the crowds who flock to these windswept chalk uplands.

INSPIRATIONAL SUSSEX

But it is walkers who are probably most at home here. Wooded in the west and bare and exposed in the east, the Downs offer miles of exhilarating walking. A bracing hike along the ridge of these hills is often accompanied by the faint tang of the sea and magnificent views of the coast and the Weald. The writer Hilaire Belloc regarded the South Downs as a national institution which lifted people's experience and understanding of them to something approaching a religious creed. He wrote of Sussex as if it were the 'crown of England'.

Another writer whose love affair with Sussex lasted a lifetime was Rudyard Kipling. Perhaps the best way to see his 'blunt, bow-headed, whale-backed Downs' is from the South Downs Way, which runs like a thread across the ridge of the hills and is one of Britain's most popular long-distance trails. However, the South Downs can be seen and admired from countless vantage points and for anyone who loves and appreciates the English landscape, a glimpse of a dramatic downland escarpment against the sky leaves a lasting impression.

SUSSEX LANDSCAPES

While some of the best walking will be found on the South Downs, there are many opportunities to explore the rest of Sussex on foot. The walks in this guide reach every corner of the county, from the gentle coastal terrain of Chichester Harbour to the glorious wooded landscape of Ashdown Forest.

Left: The cone-shaped Sugar Loaf folly built by John Fuller at Brightling (Walk 8)

The routes are designed to capture the essence and spirit of Sussex, visiting many of its famous landmarks and revealing the diversity of its splendid scenery. Every aspect of its history and geology is recorded. All that has shaped and influenced this county over the centuries is here.

WALKING IN SUSSEX & SOUTH DOWNS

It may be something of a cliché but walking remains our most popular outdoor activity. There is little to add to this statistic, save to say that one of its greatest pleasures is the opportunity to learn so much more about the countryside. A really good walk should be educational, enjoyable and informative, providing a unique insight into the changing character of our rural landscape.

Each route in this book offers a specific theme to enhance the walk, as well as lots of snippets of useful information on what to look for and what to do while you're there. The majority of the walks are circular and almost all are rural rambles, but if you prefer a city stroll, there are town walks in historic Chichester and vibrant Brighton to enjoy. Above all, take your time and enjoy the many delights that Sussex offers the explorer on foot.

WAYMARKS IN SUSSEX & SOUTH DOWNS

On your walks around Sussex, you will see various waymarking signs: blue arrows indicate bridleways, suitable for walkers, cyclists and horse-riders; yellow arrows indicate footpaths, suitable for walkers only; red arrows indicate byways, open to all traffic; and acorn markers indicate National Trails, such as the South Downs Way, and the Cleveland Way.

PUBLIC TRANSPORT Sussex is well served by public transport, making many of the walks in this guide easily accessible. The Winchelsea, Hastings, Battle, Pevensey, Arlington, Horsted Keynes, Brighton, Amberley, Arundel and Chichester walks (routes 3/4, 5, 6, 11, 17, 20, 25, 33/34, 37 and 46) start at a railway station or near to one.

For times of trains throughout Sussex call the 24-hour national train inquiry line on 08457 48 49 50; www.nationalrail.co.uk or visit www.southernrailway. com. For bus times call 0871 200 2233; www.traveline.org.uk.

Walking in Safety

All these walks are suitable for any reasonably fit person, but less experienced walkers should try the easier walks first. Route finding is usually straightforward, but you will find that an Ordnance Survey or AA walking map is a useful addition to the route maps and descriptions; recommendations can be found in the information panels.

RISKS

Although each walk here has been researched with a view to minimising the risks to the walkers who follow its route, no walk in the countryside can be considered to be completely free from risk. Walking in the outdoors will always require a degree of common sense and judgement to ensure that it is as safe as possible.

- Be particularly careful on cliff paths and in upland terrain, where the consequences of a slip can be very serious.
- Remember to check tidal conditions before walking on the seashore.
- Some sections of route are by, or cross, busy roads. Take care and remember traffic is a danger even on minor country lanes.
- Be careful around farmyard machinery and livestock, especially if you have children with you.
- Be aware of the consequences of changes in the weather and check the forecast before you set out. Carry spare clothing and a torch if you are walking in the winter months. Remember the weather can change very quickly at any time of the year, and in moorland and heathland areas, mist and fog can make route finding much harder. Don't set out in these conditions unless you are confident of your navigation skills in poor visibility. In summer remember to take account of the heat and sun; wear a hat and carry water.
- On walks away from centres of population you should carry a whistle and survival bag. If you do have an accident requiring the emergency services, make a note of your position as accurately as possible and dial 999.

COUNTRYSIDE CODE

- Be safe, plan ahead and follow any signs.
- Leave gates and property as you find them.
- Protect plants and animals and take your litter home.
- Keep dogs under close control.
- Consider other people.

For more information visit www.naturalengland.org.uk/ourwork/enjoying/countrysidecode

Overleaf: Distant view of the white cliffs of the Seven Sisters (Walk 13)

Lagoons at Rye Harbour

DISTANCE 4.5 miles (7.2km)	MINIMUM TIME 2hrs

ASCENT/GRADIENT Negligible ▲▲▲   LEVEL OF DIFFICULTY ✦✦✦

PATHS Level paths and good, clear tracks, no stiles

LANDSCAPE Mixture of shingle expanses and old gravel workings, now part of a local nature reserve

SUGGESTED MAP OS Explorer 125 Romney Marsh, Rye & Winchelsea

START/FINISH Grid reference: TQ942189

DOG FRIENDLINESS Dogs on lead within Rye Harbour Nature Reserve

PARKING Spacious free car park at Rye Harbour

PUBLIC TOILETS Rye Harbour

Turn the clock back to the dark days of World War II and you would find Rye Harbour a very different place. Blockhouses for machine guns littered the coast, and barbed wire and landmines made it a 'no go' area. During the hours of darkness, great searchlights swept across the night sky; they were particularly effective at detecting the dreaded flying bombs. Go there now and you can still identify some of these crumbling relics of war. It's a fascinating exercise to rewrite the pages of history and imagine what might have happened if enemy forces had landed on this forgotten corner of England.

NAPOLEONIC THREAT

World War II wasn't the first time the area had been under threat, however. During the Napoleonic Wars, 150 years earlier, Rye Harbour was considered an obvious target for invasion and attack when the Martello tower, seen by the car park at the start of the walk, became the first of 47 fortifications built in Sussex as a defence against the French. The tower would certainly have been a tough deterrent. The walls are nearly 12ft (4m) thick at the base, and the middle floor would have been occupied by a garrison of one officer and 24 men.

Since then, the sea has built up over half a mile (800m) of land in front of it, with violent storms dumping huge deposits of shingle on the shore every winter. Today, the little community of Rye Harbour is peaceful and yet, years after the shadows of war have passed over, it still conveys that same sense of bleak isolation. Though not as atmospheric as neighbouring shingle-strewn Dungeness, it does feel very isolated here.

Part of a designated Site of Special Scientific Interest (SSSI), and very popular with ornithologists, Rye Harbour Nature Reserve lies at the mouth of the River Rother, which forms its eastern boundary. During its early stage, the walk follows the river, and at first glance the shingle seems so bare and inhospitable that it is hard to imagine any plant could grow here. But in late May and June the beach is transformed by a colourful array of flowers. Delicate yellow horned poppies, sea kale, carpets of seaweed and countless other species of plants thrive in this habitat. Salt marsh, vegetation along the river's edge, pools and grazing marsh add to the variety, and the old gravel pits now represent an important site for nesting terns, gulls, ducks and waders.

The walk follows the coast for some time, passing the Ternery Pool, originally two separate gravel workings dug by hand early in the 20th century. It continues along the coast before heading inland to some more flooded gravel pits. Here you might easily spot gulls, grebes, cormorants, swallows and reed warblers. Turtle doves are often seen in the fields and sometimes perch in pairs on the overhead wires.

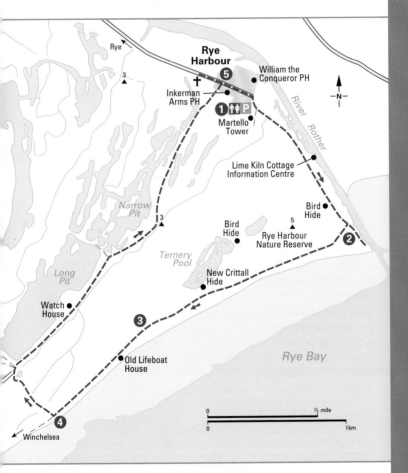

❶ Keeping the Martello Tower and the entrance to the holiday village on your right, enter Rye Harbour Nature Reserve. The Rother can be seen on the left, running parallel to the path, with a wind farm visible in the far distance. Head for Lime Kiln Cottage Information Centre and continue on the firm path, with the Rother still visible on the left. The expanse of Camber Sands, a popular holiday destination, nudges into view beyond the river mouth.

2 Near the river mouth, the route continues to the right along a private road marked with a 20mph sign, but first detour to the beach. Return to the junction and follow the private road, which has permissive access for walkers and cuts between wildlife sanctuary areas where access is not allowed. Pass the entrance to the New Crittall hide on the right. From here there are superb views over Ternery Pool, and Rye's jumble of houses can be seen sprawling over the hill in the distance. Continue west on the private road, which gradually edges nearer the shore.

3 Ahead now is the outline of the old abandoned lifeboat house and, away to the right in the distance, the unmistakable profile of Camber Castle. Keep going on the road.

4 Just after the fence on the right ends, take the waymarked footpath on the right (by a map information board, running towards a line of houses on the eastern side of the village of Winchelsea Beach) and head inland, passing a small pond on the right. Glancing back, the old lifeboat house can be seen standing out starkly against the sky. Turn right at the next junction along power lines, pass the Watch House and continue on the track as it runs alongside several lakes. Pass to the left of some dilapidated farm outbuildings and keep going along the track. Where the track forks, keep left on the main track, now leaving the power lines. The lakes are still seen on the left-hand side. Begin the approach to Rye Harbour; on the left is the spire of the church.

5 On reaching the road in the centre of the village of Rye Harbour, turn left to visit the lifeboatmen's memorial in the churchyard before heading back along the main street. Pass the Inkerman Arms and return to the car park at the start of the walk.

WHERE TO EAT AND DRINK The Inkerman Arms at Rye Harbour specialises in locally caught fresh fish. Also in Rye Harbour, the William the Conqueror pub serves food and nearby Bosun's Bite cafe offers snacks and all-day breakfasts.

WHAT TO SEE Summer visitors to Rye Harbour include common, Sandwich and little terns, as well as other ground-nesting birds such as ringed plover, oystercatcher, redshank, avocet and lapwing. This is also a notable place to observe bird migration, while in winter large numbers of wildfowl and waders gather to take full advantage of the relatively undisturbed reserve area.

WHILE YOU'RE THERE The old lifeboat station passed on the walk hasn't been used since one stormy night in November 1928 when the 17-strong crew of the *Mary Stanford* were called to rescue a leaking steamer in the English Channel, in gale force winds and huge waves. Soon afterwards, the coastguard heard the steamer was safe, but with no ship-to-shore radio available he was unable to convey a message to the lifeboat crew. The next day, the *Mary Stanford* was seen floating upside down in the water. Not one volunteer survived the tragedy. The churchyard at Rye Harbour has a memorial to the crew of the *Mary Stanford*.

Gardens at Great Dixter

DISTANCE 3 miles (4.8km)   MINIMUM TIME 1hr 30min

ASCENT/GRADIENT 98ft (30m) ▲▲▲   LEVEL OF DIFFICULTY ✚✚✚

PATHS Field paths and quiet roads, several stiles

LANDSCAPE Undulating farmland and stretches of woodland

SUGGESTED MAP OS Explorer 125 Romney Marsh, Rye & Winchelsea

START/FINISH Grid reference: TQ829245

DOG FRIENDLINESS Dog stiles near Great Dixter and on Sussex Border Path

PARKING Free car park on corner of Fullers Lane and A28, Northiam

PUBLIC TOILETS Great Dixter, seasonal opening

Deep in the tranquil, rolling countryside of East Sussex, close to the Kent border, lies the wonderful Great Dixter, one of the county's smaller and more intimate historic houses.

FAMILY THEME

Built in the mid-15th century and later restored and enlarged by Sir Edwin Lutyens, Great Dixter is a popular tourist attraction as well as a family home. These days this fine Wealden hall-house is owned and cared for by Olivia Eller and was the home of her late uncle, Christopher Lloyd, the gardening writer. It was Christopher's father, Nathaniel, who in 1910 instructed Lutyens to make major changes to Great Dixter, which at that time was in a poor state of repair. His main task was to clear the house of later alterations and, typically, the work was undertaken with great sensitivity.

While the restoration plans were taking shape, Lutyens and Lloyd also seized on the opportunity to improve and enlarge the house. A complete timber-framed yeoman's hall at Benenden in Kent, scheduled for demolition, was skilfully dismantled and moved to Great Dixter, adding an entire wing to the house.

One of Great Dixter's most striking features is the magnificent Great Hall, the largest surviving timber-framed hall in the country. Visitors never fail to be impressed by its medieval splendour. The half-timbered and plastered front and the Tudor porch also catch the eye. The contents of Great Dixter date mainly from the 17th and 18th centuries, collected over the years by Nathaniel Lloyd, and the house also contains many examples of delicately-fashioned needlework completed by his wife Daisy and their children.

IMPRESSIVE GARDENS

The gardens of Great Dixter are equally impressive. As with the house, plans for improvement were drawn up, and here Lutyens was just as inventive. He often used tiles in a decorative though practical manner, to great effect. At Great Dixter he took a chicken house with crumbling walls and transformed it into an open-sided loggia, supported by laminated tile pillars. Christopher Lloyd spent many years continuing this project, incorporating medieval buildings, establishing natural ponds and designing yew topiary. The result is one of the most exciting, colourful and constantly changing gardens of modern times.

Beginning in Northiam, the walk heads round the edge of the village before reaching the house at Great Dixter. Even out of season, when the place is closed, you gain a vivid impression of the house and its Sussex Weald setting. Passing directly in front of Great Dixter, the route then crosses rolling countryside to join the Sussex Border Path, following it all the way back to Northiam.

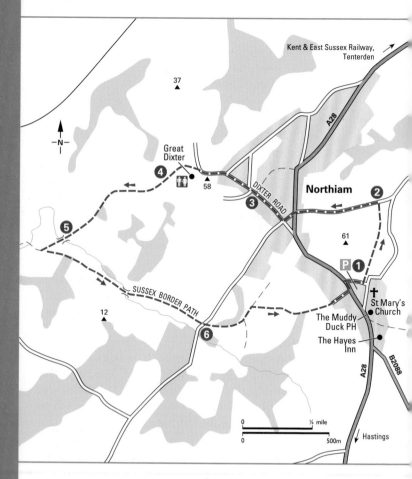

❶ Turn right out of the car park and walk along Fullers Lane towards St Mary's Church. Take the path on the left, signposted to Goddens Gill, and keep to the right edge of the field. Go through a gate in the corner; away to the right you can see an oasthouse. Make for a path on the far side of the field and follow it between fences towards a thatched cottage.

2 Go through a gate and turn left to follow the road to the A28. Bear diagonally left across the A28 and follow Thyssel Lane, signposted 'Great Dixter'. Turn right at the crossroads, following Dixter Road.

3 Pass roads called Chapel Field and Higham Lane on the left and continue to follow the signs for Great Dixter. Disregard a turning on the right (Dixter Lane) and go straight on, following a path between trees and hedges, parallel to and on the right side of the main drive to the house.

4 Head towards a cattle grid. Cross the stile just to the left of it and follow the path, signposted to Ewhurst. Follow the waymarks and keep left along the hedge. Cross a stile in the field corner and then head diagonally down the field slope to the next stile. Follow the clear path down the field slope in line with the left-hand pylon in the distance.

5 Make for a footbridge and then turn left to join the Sussex Border Path. The path skirts the field before disappearing left into some woodland. Emerging from the trees, cut straight across the next field to a footbridge. Keep the woodland on the left and look for a gap in the trees. Cross a stream to a stile and bear right. Follow the right edge of the field and keep on the Sussex Border Path until you reach the road.

6 Cross over the lane to a drive. Bear immediately left and follow the path to a stile. Pass alongside woodland and then veer slightly away from the trees to a gap in the approaching boundary (Northiam church spire is now visible ahead). Go slightly left on the path up the field slope. Take the first footpath on the right and follow it to a gap in the field corner. Cross a footbridge under the trees and continue along the right-hand edge of the next field to join a drive. Bear left and follow it to the A28. Cross over to return to the car park at Northiam.

WHERE TO EAT AND DRINK The Hayes Inn and The Muddy Duck in Northiam both open all day at weekends and serve bar food. Opposite The Hayes Inn, Will's Bakery has a tea room. When Great Dixter is open, you can buy soft drinks and basic prepacked snacks from the gift shop. There is also a picnic area.

WHAT TO SEE Visit Northiam's parish church. Not much is known of its early history, though part of it dates from the 12th century. Most of the chancel is modern. Have a look at the clock which was repaired and restored through the generosity of parishioners. A victory peal of bells rang out on 8 May 1945 – VE Day – and the names of the six bell ringers are recorded inside the church.

WHILE YOU'RE THERE Travel a mile (1.6km) or so along the A28 to take a train ride on the delightful Kent and East Sussex Railway. The railway, which opened in 1900, ran from Robertsbridge to Headcorn and was used mainly for taking farm produce to market, and for bringing in coal to drive machinery and for household fires. The coalyard at the station is still in use. The line closed to passengers in 1954 and to goods in 1961. Northiam station reopened in 1990 through the efforts of the *Challenge Anneka* television show.

Winchelsea's Land-locked Port

DISTANCE 4.5 miles (7.2km)	MINIMUM TIME 2hrs

ASCENT/GRADIENT 197ft (60m) ▲▲▲   LEVEL OF DIFFICULTY ✦✦✦

PATHS Field paths and pavements, many stiles

LANDSCAPE Mixture of marshland and undulating farmland

SUGGESTED MAP OS Explorer 124 Hastings & Bexhill or 125 Romney Marsh, Rye & Winchelsea

START/FINISH Grid reference: TQ905173

DOG FRIENDLINESS On lead near birding hide and across farmland

PARKING Roadside parking near St Thomas's Church at Winchelsea

PUBLIC TOILETS Winchelsea

The story of unlucky Winchelsea is fascinating; surely nowhere else in the country can have fallen victim to fate in quite the same way. Looking at the sleepy town today, it seems hard to believe it was once a thriving port, one of the most important on the south coast.

CINQUE PORT

This delightful little town, one of the seven Cinque Ports, became stranded when the sea receded, exposing a stretch of fertile marshland. Now it lies more than a mile (1.6km) inland.

But Winchelsea's run of bad luck did not begin here. The current town replaced Old Winchelsea in the late 13th century, when it was inundated by the sea and swept away by a great storm in 1287. The old town now lies beneath the English Channel, somewhere out in Rye Bay. As the water encroached, the inhabitants built new homes on the hilltop, establishing themselves on higher ground before the disaster finally took hold.

The new town was conceived and sited personally by Edward I, and, with its regular grid pattern, has long been acknowledged as perhaps the first example of medieval English town planning. Only a dozen of the proposed 39 grid squares were ever completed and the ambitious plans for the new Winchelsea were eventually abandoned. Three gates, part of the original fortification, still survive, including Strand Gate with its four round towers. Many of the buildings seen today date from the 17th and 18th centuries, but a number are built over earlier medieval wine cellars.

Winchelsea's bad luck continued through the Middle Ages when the town came under constant attack from the French, suffering heavy damage. The church, much of which was destroyed during the last raid of 1449, includes the tomb of Gervase Alard, England's first admiral, as well as various monuments and a wall painting from the 14th century.

Before starting the walk, take a tour round the town – the views from Strand Gate out towards the Channel are impressive. This is a walk of two extremes. From Winchelsea's lofty vantage point, you'll descend to a bare, rather featureless landscape, skirting a flat expanse of water meadows known as Pett Level. The return leg is more undulating, with good views both of the coast and Winchelsea's unspoiled hilltop setting.

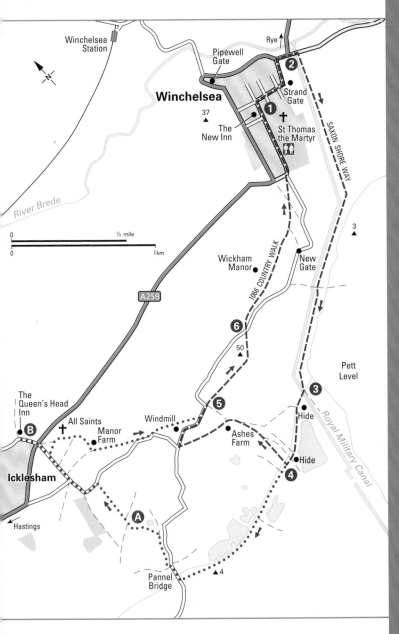

1 With The New Inn on your left and partly ruined St Thomas's church on the right, follow the road round the right-hand bend. Head down to Strand Gate and then take the road to the junction with the A259. Turn right and follow the pavement along here.

2 When the road bends left, turn right into a road signed Winchelsea Beach. Just after crossing the Royal Military Canal, turn right. Follow the tow path across this empty landscape. At the first path junction, avoid the concrete footbridge. Eventually, the canal begins to curve left.

3 Just after the next stile, turn right over the footbridge, then take the left-hand footbridge and proceed alongside a water channel. Pass a birding hide and continue along the path.

4 After the next hide, cross a footbridge, keep right on the other side, then soon fork left and follow the path through the reedbeds. Begin a moderate climb and head towards a house. Keep to the left of it and follow the path through the trees. This veers right in front of some private gates and up some steps to a stile; turn left along the field-edge to another stile. Cross a drive, go through a gate and straight across the field to a stile, then continue between fences. Skirt the field to the next stile and exit to the road. Keep right here, signposted 'Winchelsea', and pass below the hilltop windmill, soon joining the 1066 Country Walk as it comes in from the left and continues along the road.

5 Go straight ahead over a stile when the lane bends left, cross the field to a stile, and keep along the left edge of two fields. Continue ahead, pass an old pill box and head down the gentle field slope.

6 Exit onto a road and turn right along it for a few paces to a stile on the left. Bear right, still on the 1066 Country Walk, and cross the next stile. Keep to the right of Wickham Manor and look for a stile in the far boundary. Cross the drive to a stile and keep ahead across the field to a stile and gate in the bottom left corner to the left of the medieval New Gate. Follow the 1066 Country Walk waymarks. The path veers left of this hummocky field, eventually crossing a pair of stiles up on the right. Bear left and begin a moderate ascent to a stone stile beside a large remnant of medieval wall. Turn right at the road, follow it round to the left and return to the centre of Winchelsea.

WHAT TO SEE The Royal Military Canal runs below Winchelsea and extends for 25 miles (40.5km). Constructed at the beginning of the 19th century, its purpose was to protect the exposed southeast coast from invasion by Napoleon's forces. William Cobbett mentions the canal in his *Rural Rides*, wondering how a 30ft (9m) wide ditch could possibly deter troops who had managed to cross the Rhine and the Danube. The Saxon Shore Way follows the tow path.

WHILE YOU'RE THERE Visit the Winchelsea Court Hall Museum, which highlights over 700 years of the Cinque Port's history with models, maps, pictures, artefacts and memorabilia.

Winchelsea and Icklesham

DISTANCE 6.25 miles (10km)	MINIMUM TIME 3hrs

ASCENT/GRADIENT 246ft (75m) ▲▲▲   LEVEL OF DIFFICULTY ✦✦✦

PATHS Field paths and quiet roads, many stiles

LANDSCAPE Valley terrain and undulating farmland

SEE MAP AND INFORMATION PANEL FOR WALK 3

Keep walking ahead at Point ❹ and follow the track along the water channel, leaving the track where it bends left, and crossing a stile. On reaching the road, turn right. Cross Pannel Bridge and just past the drive to Little Pannel Farm go up some steps. Bear right parallel with the road and take the second path left, soon turning left at a T-junction to pass to the left of a pond, Point ❹.

Avoid turns to the left; the path bends right to cross a gulley; on the other side, immediately fork right and rise to a T-junction by a field, with a house visible ahead. Take the stile ahead and cross to the next stile, alongside orchards, then turn left on the road to the next junction.

Keep forward and walk along Workhouse Lane to the village of Icklesham, crossing the busy A259 to reach The Queen's Head Inn, Point ❸. From here retrace your steps back to Workhouse Lane, pass the village hall

and then turn left to join the 1066 Country Walk. Pass Icklesham's All Saints Church, which has fine Norman arches inside, and continue on the enclosed path to Manor Farm.

Take the grass track to the right of the drive, near the oasthouses at the farm, after which briefly join the drive and immediately take the stile on the left. Go along the fence towards a windmill, carrying on along an enclosed path, then turning right to a lane. Turn left and, when the lane bends right after a few steps, cross the stile on the corner and continue along the 1066 Country Walk.

Follow the path up the grassy slope and keep to the left of the windmill, which was used by Paul McCartney as a recording studio. A view of the Pannel Valley and the coast opens up. Drop down to a stile and some cottages and turn left at the road. Follow Points ❺ and ❻ back to Winchelsea.

WHERE TO EAT AND DRINK The 18th-century New Inn at Winchelsea offers food and has a beer garden. Also in Winchelsea is Winchelsea Farm Kitchen, a delicatessen with a coffee shop attached. The Queen's Head Inn in Icklesham has traditional pub food, a wide selection of ales and a garden with sweeping views towards Rye.

Overleaf: Wooden net sheds on the shore at Hastings (Walk 5)

Hastings Old Town and Hill

DISTANCE 4 miles (6.4km)	**MINIMUM TIME** 2hrs 30min

ASCENT/GRADIENT 328ft (100m) ▲▲▲	**LEVEL OF DIFFICULTY** ✦✦✦

PATHS Tracks, minor roads and coastal paths

LANDSCAPE High ground overlooking coast, with glens revealing layers of sandstone

SUGGESTED MAP OS Explorer 124 Hastings & Bexhill

START/FINISH Grid reference: TQ828094

DOG FRIENDLINESS Return walk, along coast path, is ideal for dogs off lead

PARKING Pay-and-display car park at Roc-a-Nore Road, Hastings

PUBLIC TOILETS In Hastings, by East Cliff cliff railway

Hastings has a real smack of the sea, with seagulls wheeling around fishing boats drawn up on the beach, known as the Stade, and a hugely characterful Old Town. Occupying a valley just to the east of the main part of town, this is a fascinating maze of tiny alleys, lanes and stepped paths with tiny cottage gardens and buildings spanning several centuries. Look out, for example, for the tiny Piece of Cheese House at 10 Starr Cottages (just off All Saints Street), named for its resemblance to a wedge of cheese, both in shape and colour. The town is familiar to many as the backdrop of the TV series *Foyle's War*.

The western part of Hastings includes the predominantly Victorian resort town and the area of St Leonards, dominated by a huge apartment block erected in the 1930s. Known as Marine Court, it was designed to resemble an ocean liner.

Hastings' two town museums are both free to enter: one is in the High Street in the Old Town, while the other occupies a larger building in the newer part of town and contains the sumptuously ornate Durbar Hall, erected for the Indian and Colonial Exhibition in 1886.

THE STADE

The Stade is home to Europe's largest beach-launched fishing fleet, and makes for a pleasant stroll, with its photogenic array of lobster pots, weather-beaten craft and fishing nets hanging out to dry. The net shops, which stand near the boats on the beach, are not really shops at all but huts for storing fishing nets and tackle. The huts, intentionally tall and narrow to reduce ground rent, are found only in Hastings. Two of them are often opened up for visitors to see; one of them, known as Half Sovereign Cottage, is formed of half a boat. Alongside them, the Jerwood Gallery houses a notable collection of modern British art in a sleek modern building clad with black ceramic tiles, designed to blend with the neighbouring net shops.

A TOWN OF TWO CLIFF RAILWAYS

Hastings most unusually has the distinction of having two cliff railways. One ascends West Hill, reaching an expanse of lawn close to the ruins of Hastings Castle, part of which has crumbled over the cliff edge. On the East Hill is Britain's steepest cliff railway; the journey is simple, short and straightforward and the views are magnificent. It takes you up the start of the walk (note it does not operate on weekdays in winter), above which are the only sandstone cliffs in Southeast England; they have quite a different look from anywhere else in the region. Hastings is fortunate indeed to have scenery of this quality on its doorstep.

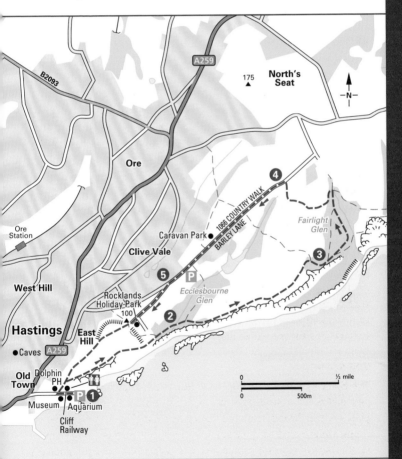

1 Turn left out of the car park, along Roc-a-Nore Road, to the East Hill cliff railway. Either take the ride to the top, or walk up. (If you prefer to walk, carry on along the road a few paces past the Dolphin pub, then right up Tamarisk Steps; at the top turn left on the road, then right up more steps to ascend to the upper cliff railway station.) Keep right up more steps, and follow the Saxon Shore Way along the southern slopes of East Hill, with the sea on your right. Pass a beacon on your left and keep to the right, eventually passing a sign for Ecclesbourne Glen (lower).

2 Descend almost to sea level and then climb out of the glen via a flight of steps. At the top of the steps, continue ahead, with scrub and gorse on the right now blocking out views of the sea; ignore any paths to the left. Drop steeply into Fairlight Glen.

3 At the bottom of Fairlight Glen, turn left at bollard 16 just before a stream – signposted Barley Lane – up the glen. Ignore steps leading down to the right and, just after, turn sharp left at a junction by bollard 15 (ahead here is a map). Follow the track out of the woods, keeping forward at gates.

4 Reach Barley Lane and turn left along it. Carry on past a caravan park and Barley Lane car park.

5 Just after passing a path on the right, signposted Harold Road, fork left into Rocklands Lane (with a 15mph speed limit sign). Soon you gain a view over the sprawling jumble of rooftops, with rows of terraced houses scattered over the slopes and hillsides. This is residential Hastings. Pass to the right of the entrance of Rocklands Holiday Park and keep on the upper track at the fork. Cross the grassy expanse of East Hill by aiming slightly right. Much of the town can be seen down below you, creating an impressive picture. Keep well to the right of the beacon passed earlier and reach the top of the East Hill cliff railway, either travelling on it to return or taking the steps just to the right to zigzag to the bottom.

WHERE TO EAT AND DRINK Hastings Old Town has a comprehensive choice, with the Lord Nelson and Dolphin pubs near the cliff railway, the Cinque Ports Inn in All Saints Street and several options in the High Street.

WHAT TO SEE On East Hill above Hastings is a beacon, erected in 1988 to commemorate the 400th anniversary of the Spanish Armada. The original beacon was found at nearby North Seat. The hill also marks the site of an Iron Age settlement, established by Celts in about 40 BC. Defended by earth banks and the cliff face, the site occupied a prominent position overlooking a natural harbour.

WHILE YOU'RE THERE Make a point of visiting the Fishermen's Museum in Roc-a-Nore Road. It illustrates the history and tradition of fishing on this coast over the centuries. In the Middle Ages, Hastings was an important harbour, and today fishing is still a major industry here. The town has the largest beach-launched fishing fleet in Europe. Next to it are the Shipwreck Museum, with a fascinating array of objects and craft found locally, and the Blue Reef aquarium, where you can walk through a glass tunnel beneath a spectacular 'reef pool' – home to sharks, rays, crabs and starfish. Visit the acre of subterranean tunnels and caverns at the Smugglers Adventure in Hastings Old Town and experience smuggling as it was over 200 years ago.

Battle – Britain's Most Famous Battlefield

DISTANCE 5 miles (8km)   MINIMUM TIME 2hrs 30min

ASCENT/GRADIENT 448ft (137m) ▲▲▲   LEVEL OF DIFFICULTY ✦✦✦

PATHS Field and woodland paths, some road walking, several stiles

LANDSCAPE Gently undulating farmland and woodland

SUGGESTED MAP OS Explorer 124 Hastings & Bexhill

START/FINISH Grid reference: TQ747156

DOG FRIENDLINESS Enclosed woodland paths and stretches of 1066 Country Walk suitable for dogs off lead

PARKING Car park at Battle Abbey (fee)

PUBLIC TOILETS Mount Street car park in Battle; Battle Abbey

If one date from England's past stands out more than any other, it is surely 1066. One of the most important and significant events in British history, the Battle of Hastings represents a defining moment.

BLOODY BATTLE

On the battlefield you can still sense something of that momentous day when William, Duke of Normandy, defeated Harold and his army and became William the Conqueror of England. See the spot where Harold is believed to have fallen and, with a little imagination, you can picture the bloody events that led to his defeat.

William began by positioning his army on a hill about 400yds (365m) to the south of the English army, massed on a higher hilltop. Harold and his men fortified their formidable position and, following abortive uphill charges on the English shield-wall, the Normans withdrew, unable to breach the defences. It looked for a time as if victory was within Harold's grasp – until William rallied his men and executed two successful strategies. One was to instruct his bowmen to shoot their arrows indiscriminately into the air, though William had no idea that one of them would (so one version of the tale says) hit Harold in the eye, fatally wounding him. William's other plan was to create the impression that his armies were fleeing the battlefield. Sensing victory, the English gave chase, but the Normans rounded on them and won the battle. William marched victoriously to London where, on Christmas Day, in Westminster Abbey, he was duly crowned King of England.

WILLIAM'S PROMISE

Before the Battle of Hastings, William vowed that if God gave him victory that day, he would build an abbey on the site of the battle at

Senlac Field. This he did, with the high altar set up on the spot where Harold died.

Little of the church remains today. The abbey, thought to have been completed before William died, was significantly enlarged and improved in later years. However, after the Dissolution of the Monasteries, much of it was converted into a private house by Sir Anthony Browne, Henry VIII's Master of Horse. Today, Battle Abbey is in the care of English Heritage and a popular tourist attraction.

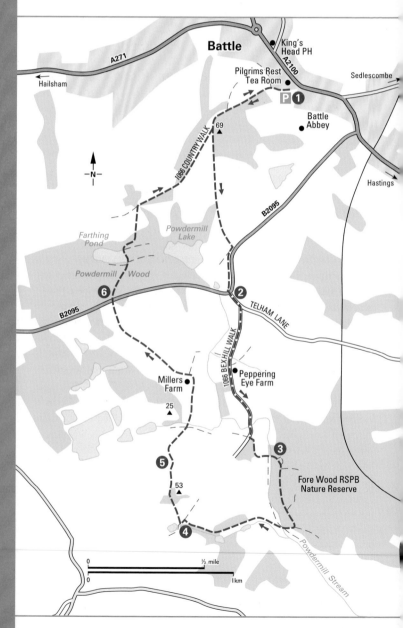

1 Turn left out of the car park and follow the track to a gate. Keep left along the bridleway beside woodland, the path swinging left to a fingerpost and junction of paths. Bear off left with the 1066 Bexhill Walk marker and walk down the field-edge and through two gates. Keep ahead, soon to cross a drive via a stile and a gate, and follow the fenced path along the field-edge high above the road.

2 Cross the B2095 (take care – dangerous bend), walk along Telham Lane and take the private road right towards Peppering Eye Farm. After the farm, keep to the metalled drive for 0.5 miles (0.8km), passing under power cables and crossing a stream to ascend to a junction of paths by Powdermill Cottage. Turn left along a track through the trees to a gate, and bear off left with the waymarker across the centre of a field.

3 Cross a footbridge to enter Fore Wood RSPB Nature Reserve. Bear right and follow the yellow-arrowed route through the wood, ignoring a path on the left and turning right at the far side of the wood where the path curves left at a bench. Go left at the fingerpost, cross a footbridge and follow the path right through scrub, parallel with the stream. On reaching an open field, keep left around the field-edge to leave at the top left corner, then carry on along a path in a semi-wooded area past three oak trees and with a pond just visible down to the left. This passes another larger pond, then soon emerges into a field, keeping ahead along the field-edge.

4 Reach a junction of tracks and bear left, then immediately right at a fork, curving left around a pond to emerge from the woodland by a waymarker close to pheasant pens. Turn right up the grassy bank, soon enter woodland and continue to a stile and footbridge. Turn left to another stile, then right along the field-edge passing a pond, and head across the field in line with distant barns, passing beneath power cables.

5 Beyond the next gateway, bear diagonally right downhill across the field to a gate and go forward up a track. Just before the barns, climb the stile on the right to follow the arrowed path around Millers Farm to reach a gate just before the brick farmhouse. Rejoin the track and follow it for 0.5 miles (0.8km).

6 Cross a road, pass beside a gate and follow the path through Powdermill Wood. Cross a footbridge and go along a fence by Farthing Pond, at the end of which immediately fork left uphill along a narrow path through coppice woodland to a kissing-gate. Cross the field, aiming to the right of a cottage to reach a kissing-gate. Turn right along a track, go through a gate and follow the 1066 Walk uphill through a field. Retrace your outward route back to the car park.

WHERE TO EAT AND DRINK There are several pubs, restaurants and tea rooms in Battle, including the 15th-century Kings Head, the Pilgrims Rest tea room and the Battle Deli and Coffee Shop.

WHAT TO SEE Fore Wood RSPB Nature Reserve is home to dragonflies, damselflies, nuthatches, treecreepers and woodpeckers, with rare mosses and ferns thriving in the shaded valleys.

Rudyard Kipling's Bateman's at Burwash

DISTANCE 4.75 miles (7.7km)	MINIMUM TIME 2hrs
ASCENT/GRADIENT 345ft (105m) ▲▲▲	LEVEL OF DIFFICULTY ✚✚✚

PATHS Field and woodland paths, stretches of minor road, several stiles

LANDSCAPE Rolling, semi-wooded countryside of the Dudwell Valley

SUGGESTED MAP OS Explorers 124 Hastings & Bexhill, 136 The High Weald

START/FINISH Grid reference: TQ674246

DOG FRIENDLINESS Dogs on lead in vicinity of Bateman's and Park Farm and on stretches of farmland. Off lead on woodland paths and tracks. Bateman's has a dog crèche

PARKING Free car park off A265 in Burwash village

PUBLIC TOILETS At car park

Bateman's was Rudyard Kipling's refuge from the world. This was his spiritual home and it was here that he found true happiness. Touring the house and exploring the garden, it's not difficult to see why he fell in love with the place.

KIPLING'S HOME

Bateman's is a charming family home, small and intimate, occupying a peaceful setting in a secluded valley. Built by a local ironmaster in 1634, the house lies about 25 miles (40km) to the northeast of Kipling's old home at Rottingdean. Kipling purchased the house in 1902 and, now in the care of the National Trust, it remains much as it was in Kipling's day.

It was here, in his book-lined study, that Kipling wrote some of his most famous works, including *Puck of Pook's Hill*. The house, and the peace and tranquillity of the surrounding countryside, greatly inspired him, and over the years he acquired more and more land so that he could write and relax away from public scrutiny; 'We have loved it ever since our first sight of it', he wrote later.

ROSE GARDEN

Kipling loved the garden just as much as the house, designing and landscaping it and putting his own mark on it. He planted yew hedges to give him more privacy and even erected a pear arch. Visitors to Bateman's can see the results of his labours, and can also take a stroll through the beautiful rose garden which he designed after being awarded the Nobel Prize for Literature in 1907.

Kipling relished his privacy, although he liked to socialise, and was known for his curious but discreet manner of asking guests to leave.

He would lead them past the garden sundial, which indicated that it was later than it really was, and hence suggest that they should make their farewells. He was also a keen motorist. He bought a Rolls-Royce, which he maintained was the only car he could afford, and embarked on many journeys, travelling abroad and visiting his old school in Devon. He recorded his travels in detail and even dispatched reports and memos to the Automobile Association.

This glorious valley walk passes Bateman's near the start and then again towards the finish. A tour of the house and gardens reveals how the National Trust has preserved the character and integrity of the man, as well as the atmosphere of the place. Kipling died in 1936, after 34 years at Bateman's. Looking at the house today, it is not difficult to see why he described it as 'a real house in which to settle down for keeps...a good and peaceable place'.

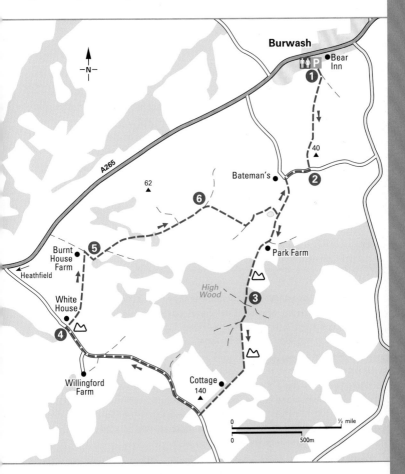

❶ Make for the footpath behind the toilets. Follow the path down the slope and at a junction of paths cross the plank bridge and gate on the right. Continue ahead, making for the next gate and keep the boundary hedge on your right. Look for a stile on the right and then head diagonally down the field. Make for a signpost in the field corner, follow the left-hand field-edge to a stile and exit to the road. (Note this point; you will return to it later.)

2 Turn right and follow the lane along to Bateman's. Keep left in front of the house itself and proceed past some houses. At Park Farm ignore the arrowed gate on the left and continue through the farm, then bear off left uphill through to the edge of some woodland to a gate. Head up the field slope, keeping the trees on your immediate right. Look for a gate and bridleway post on the right, passing through the wood.

3 Bear left at a T-junction with a track, then immediately right and follow the bridleway, keeping left at the fork. Pass a solitary cottage and walk along to the road. Turn right downhill, eventually passing the entrance to Willingford Farm and then, after the road crosses a stream, start to climb quite steeply.

4 Just before a small white house on the right, go right through a kissing gate and head diagonally across a large field; soon the buildings of Burnt House Farm come into view. Go through a small metal gate (the left-hand of two gates) in the field corner, carry on below the buildings through waymarked gates, and then walk along the top left side of a field.

5 At a junction of waymarked paths keep forward, ignoring the path to the right. Carry on along the edge of the next field, past a metal water tank and down through a belt of woodland to a field, and head down just to left of the chimney of a house. Turn right along a surfaced lane which very quickly becomes a grassy track, passing some dilapidated farm outbuildings.

6 Cross over a stile by a gate and keep right here. Look for another stile near the end of the field, turn left and then skirt round the edge of the field. Veer over to a stile towards the far end, cross a footbridge and turn left. Follow the path over a sluice, past a pond and a cottage, bearing right to a track. Turn left and head back to Bateman's, and retrace your steps to Burwash.

WHERE TO EAT AND DRINK In Burwash, The Bear Inn has been in business for more than 300 years, whilst The Bell Inn is a delightful 17th-century inn with a log fire and a heavily beamed ceiling. Close by is the Rose and Crown. Burwash also has the Lime Tree Tearooms. Bateman's includes a popular tea room.

WHAT TO SEE Neighbour to Bateman's is the picturesque village of Burwash, which lies on a ridge between the rivers Rother and Dudwell. There are many white weatherboarded cottages and various beautiful tile-hung buildings, making it typical of East Sussex. The war memorial by the church was unveiled by Rudyard Kipling and his son is one of those commemorated. The church has a fine Norman tower with a shingled spire.

WHILE YOU'RE THERE Make a point of visiting the watermill at Bateman's. The 18th-century mill, which was restored by dedicated volunteers, grinds corn for flour; attached to the wheel is one of the earliest water-driven turbines, installed by Rudyard Kipling to generate electricity for the house. There is a delightful walk from the house to the watermill on the River Dudwell.

Brightling's Folly Trail

DISTANCE 5 miles (8km)	MINIMUM TIME 2hrs 30min
ASCENT/GRADIENT 197ft (60m) ▲▲▲	LEVEL OF DIFFICULTY ✦✦✦

PATHS Parkland paths, woodland bridleways and lanes

LANDSCAPE Parkland and dense woodland

SUGGESTED MAP OS Explorer 124 Hastings & Bexhill

START/FINISH Grid reference: TQ683210

DOG FRIENDLINESS Off lead in woodland, but heed signs

PARKING Limited spaces by phone box near Brightling church. Avoid times of church services. Alternatively, park at Darwell

PUBLIC TOILETS None on route

Scattered around the peaceful village of Brightling are the monuments and follies created by former resident John 'Mad Jack' Fuller – a man for whom the word 'eccentric' is something of an understatement. Long after Fuller's death in 1834, his name lives on, as does his reputation as a wilful, autocratic and larger-than-life character who embraced a wide range of interests and became a renowned patron of the arts.

FULLER'S FORTUNE SECURE

John Fuller was born in 1757, the son of a Hampshire rector. The family made its money from the Sussex iron industry, allowing the young John a privileged upbringing. He attended Eton and on his 20th birthday inherited the family fortune and its estates. His future was secure.

He came close to marriage in his 30s but his proposal was declined. Fuller remained a bachelor for the rest of his life, at first throwing himself headlong into politics. He stood for Parliament on several occasions and eventually became the Honourable Member for East Sussex. But Fuller was no ordinary MP. He was the stuff of which legends are made – swearing at the Speaker of the House of Commons, thundering down from London in a carriage with footmen armed to the teeth with pistols and drawn swords, refusing a peerage, consuming three bottles of port a day and engaging in reckless, impossible wagers.

'MAD JACK'

It was hardly surprising that he became known as 'Mad Jack'. With his 22-stone (140kg) frame and loud, bellowing voice, Fuller often induced fear in the strongest of souls. In fact, his quick temper and unpredictable nature eventually ruined his prospects of climbing the political ladder. After insulting the Speaker he was forcibly removed from the chamber by the Sergeant at Arms and ordered to apologise.

He did not stand again for Parliament and quickly became disillusioned with politics, instead focusing his attention on folly-building.

Explore Brightling and the surrounding countryside and you will see Fuller's follies everywhere, keeping alive his memory, reflecting his quirky nature and his taste for the absurd. Even his final resting place seems wildly over the top. This, his final folly, is a sandstone pyramid mausoleum erected in Brightling churchyard, where the walk begins. For many years people genuinely believed that Fuller had been interred in an upright position, dressed for dinner, holding a bottle of claret and wearing a top hat. When the tomb was eventually opened for restoration work, the rumours proved to be unfounded, though, given his exuberant personality, it would not be surprising if the gossip had been true.

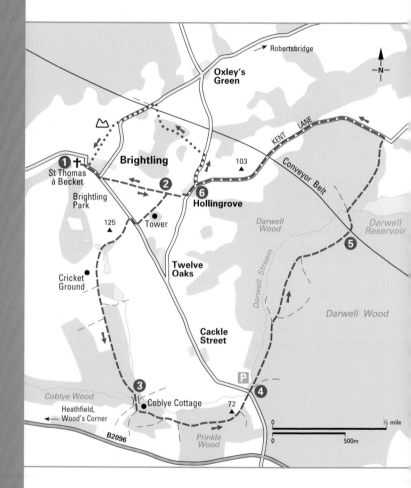

1 Walk through the churchyard opposite Wealden House, down to the road. Turn right to reach Brightling

Park and make for a turning on the left, signposted 'Robertsbridge'. Go through a galvanised kissing gate by the junction and follow the clear path across the fields and between fences to a footpath junction and sign.

2 Turn right here and follow the field-edge towards the Tower. Cross a stile on the right, cut through the trees past the Tower and descend the field slope to the stile and road. Bear right for a few paces, turning left by the barns and outbuildings of Ox Lodge. Cut between ponds and lakes and look for a cricket ground by the track. The Temple can be seen on the right. Pass a turning to some farm outbuildings and continue on the main bridleway, signed Coblye, keeping ahead when it forks. Cut through an area of pheasant-rearing woodland and descend.

3 Cross a footbridge, climb past Coblye Cottage on the left, then fork left and keep to the main track through Prinkle Wood, ignoring paths left and right. Eventually reach a waymarker post and gate, exit the wood and follow the track downhill to a gate and road. Cross over.

4 From the car park with the road behind you, take the left-hand bridle track and, when it eventually forks, keep to the right. Follow bridleway signs. When the track swings sharply to the right at a hairpin bend, look for a bridleway sign on the left and follow the path through the wood.

5 On emerging from the trees, cross over a pipe enclosing a conveyor belt linking Mountfield and Brightling gypsum mines. Follow the track to the left and then veer right after a few steps at the fork. Cross over the Darwell Stream and bear right, following the woodland path up through the trees to the road. Turn right to glimpse Darwell Reservoir and turn left to continue the walk. Follow Kent Lane, recross the conveyor belt and make for the hamlet of Hollingrove. On the right here is an old chapel, which is now a house.

6 Keep left at the junction and walk along the lane for a short distance, passing Whitehouse. Take the stony track on the right and veer left after a few paces in front of a part tile-hung house (AEF 1840 on the front). Walk along to the turning for the Tower, visited earlier on the walk, retrace your steps across the fields and follow the road back to Brightling church.

WHAT TO SEE In the middle of Brightling Park, landscaped by 'Capability' Brown, stands the Grecian-style Rotunda Temple, a circular domed building. It may have been used as a hide-out for smugglers or a store for contraband. Alternatively, Fuller might have built it for gambling sessions or entertaining ladies. Darwell Reservoir is managed as a trout fishery and is popular with anglers and ornithologists.

WHILE YOU'RE THERE Have a look at the pyramid mausoleum and the Parish Church of St Thomas à Becket. There's plenty to see and an audio guide enables you to pick out the various features. John Fuller was a generous benefactor and his donations included the provision of a barrel organ in 1820. Near the start of the walk, close to the road, is one of Fuller's more accessible follies. The circular Tower, dating back to the 1820s, is a two-storey, stone-built construction with a Gothic entrance and a top surrounded by battlements. It is suggested that Fuller erected it so he could see Bodiam Castle, which he later bought for £3,000 to save it from demolition.

Around Brightling Woodlands

DISTANCE 6 miles (9.7km)   MINIMUM TIME 3hrs

ASCENT/GRADIENT 312ft (95m) ▲▲▲   LEVEL OF DIFFICULTY ✚✚✚

PATHS Woodland, pasture and high ground, good views, several stiles

SEE MAP AND INFORMATION PANEL FOR WALK 8

To extend Walk 8 a little way further, turn right at Point **6**, by the former chapel, and follow the lane north. Pass Hollytree Cottage, a handsome timber-and-thatch house, and turn immediately left. After a few paces you reach a stile. Head diagonally right across the pasture, making for a curtain of woodland. Look for a stile in a gap in the trees and undergrowth, and go down the steps to a footbridge over a stream.

This is a very pleasant sheltered spot, the tree cover providing cooling shade on a warm day. Cross the bridge and bear right. Follow the path, which bends right and immediately left, then a few paces after, fork right on a path. 50yds (46m) before a gate ahead out of the woods, take care to fork right through the woods down another path, leaving the woods at a barrier and rising to go over the gypsum mine conveyor belt, its low rumble often audible as you approach it.

After crossing the bridge, veer left to a stile as the track bends right. Cross the pasture to the next stile by a galvanised gate and exit to the road. Turn left and follow the road, passing a footpath on the right. Recross the conveyor belt and as the road begins to curve left, look for a stile and footpath sign on the right. Follow the path up the rise, to reach an open grassy strip with power lines. Turn left, then follow the right edge of a field.

Glance back on this stretch to enjoy a superb view of rural Sussex. The trees of Darwell Wood cloak the landscape but somewhere deep within them lies the bridleway which forms the middle section of the main walk. Leave the field by the far right-hand corner. Turn left and follow the path to a gate and drive. Bear right and return to the centre of Brightling, emerging at the road by the village hall near the phone box and the church.

WHERE TO EAT AND DRINK There are no refreshment facilities on either walk. When you finish your walk, try the Swan Inn at Wood's Corner, to the southwest of Brightling. A good range of food and drink is available and the pub has a cosy, welcoming atmosphere.

History and Science at Herstmonceux

DISTANCE 3 miles (4.8km)   MINIMUM TIME 1hr 30min

ASCENT/GRADIENT 153ft (47m) ▲▲▲   LEVEL OF DIFFICULTY ✦✦✦

PATHS Woodland and field paths, country lanes

LANDSCAPE Wood, farmland and parkland on edge of Pevensey Levels

SUGGESTED MAP OS Explorer 124 Hastings & Bexhill

START/FINISH Grid reference: TQ654103

DOG FRIENDLINESS On a lead in woodland. Off lead on 1066 Country Walk

PARKING Small lay-by on Wartling Road, south of A271, near entrance to The Observatory Science Centre

PUBLIC TOILETS Castle and Science Centre, seasonal opening (visitors only)

A romantic-looking 15th-century moated castle set in beautiful parkland and superb Elizabethan gardens, Herstmonceux perfectly captures the essence of medieval England – although it is actually inspired by the French châteaux of the period. At the time William, Duke of Normandy, marched through Sussex to do battle with Harold and his Saxon army, Herstmonceux was probably no more than a small manor. *Herst* is a Saxon word meaning 'clearing' and *Monceux* comes from Drogo de Monceux, a relative of William. The land later passed to the Fiennes family, ancestors of Ralph Fiennes and his brother Joseph, two of Britain's leading modern film actors.

SHAM CASTLE

It was in 1441 that Sir Roger de Fiennes, treasurer of the royal household, applied for a royal licence to build a castle here – though he wanted to use it to entertain his friends, not to defend his country. When first erected it was the only building in England of its size to be formed of bricks. Herstmonceux is also perhaps the first example of a sham – a country pile disguised as a castle.

Much of the interior was demolished in 1776 to build nearby Herstmonceux Place, which is glimpsed from a distance on this walk, and which from 1807 to 1819 was the residence of Thomas Read Kemp, the founder of Kemp Town in Brighton. By Victorian times, the castle was little more than a romantic ruin.

CENTRE OF SCIENCE

Herstmonceux Castle was rebuilt in 1911, and in 1947 became the home of the Royal Greenwich Observatory, which had been established on the east side of London in 1646 under Charles II with the purpose of recording the positions of the stars as a navigation aid to sailors. Due to increasing light pollution, the Observatory relocated again in 1984, this time to the top of an extinct volcano on La Palma in the Canary Islands. The castle and grounds were bought by Queen's University, Ontario, for use as an international study centre, a role that continues to this day. During late August, the whole site is transformed by a huge medieval festival featuring knights in armour, falconry displays, jousting tournaments, strolling minstrels and jesters.

In sharp contrast to the castle are the buildings of The Observatory Science Centre next door. These famous green domes still house large telescopes, and it is possible to come on open evenings and see the night sky close-up.

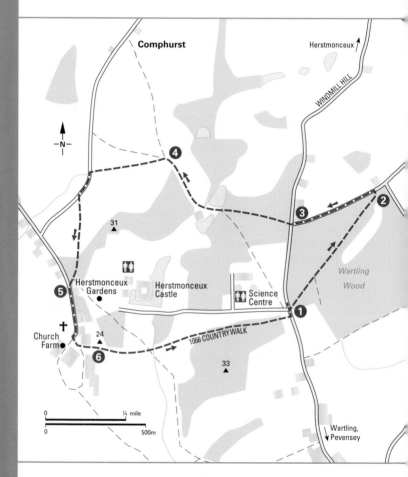

1 From the lay-by, make for the entrance to the Science Centre, cross Wartling Road to a stile and enter the extensive woodland. Turn left at a T-junction by a signpost and continue on the straight footpath, picking your way through the trees.

2 Eventually reach a stile. Turn left, then immediately left into Wood Lane.

Follow the road, with the coppiced woodland and an ancient boundary bank seen on the left.

3 Reach a road junction and cross over to a signposted bridleway. Continue ahead through the woodland on a path that is initially concrete. Just after a path joins from the left, pass a reed-clogged lake (one of a chain of ponds), and carry on along the wide path between the trees.

4 Emerge into farmland by a galvanised gate, with a view of 18th-century Herstmonceux Place. Immediately go left through a second gate then head across the field to reach a track. Keep left and, after about 60yds (55m), veer left at a waymark by a concrete trough. Cross the field, heading up the slope to reach a line of trees. Look for a gate, avoid the immediate fork to the left,

and follow the level path through the woodland. Cross over a path and then continue walking along the bridleway.

5 Reach the road and turn left. Just past Herstmonceux church, turn left on the 1066 Country Walk and follow the concrete drive to a gate to the left of the entrance to Church Farmhouse.

6 Cross over a tarmac lane serving the study centre and, as you descend the slope, the domes of the old observatory begin to peep into view above the trees. Make for the next galvanised gate and an impressive view of Herstmonceux Castle over on the left. Cross a footpath to another gate. Begin a gradual, though not particularly steep, climb and continue on the 1066 Country Walk as it runs hard by the Science Centre boundary. Follow the woodland path to the road, turn left and return to the lay-by.

WHERE TO EAT AND DRINK The Lamb at nearby Wartling is an attractive 17th-century free house and restaurant. There is a tea room in the grounds of Herstmonceux Castle and plenty of picnic space at the Science Centre and Discovery Park.

WHAT TO SEE Herstmonceux church, about 2 miles (3.2km) from the village centre and overlooking Pevensey Levels, stands on a wooded rise opposite one of the entrances to Herstmonceux Castle. The church is dedicated to All Saints, indicating that it is probably of Saxon origin. As you join the 1066 Country Walk, you cannot fail to spot the white-domed satellite laser ranger, which belongs to the Royal Greenwich Observatory.

WHILE YOU'RE THERE Visit the grounds of Herstmonceux Castle to see the walled garden (from before 1570), a herb garden, woodland sculptures and a folly. Walks take you to the remains of a 300-year-old sweet chestnut avenue, a rhododendron garden and a waterfall. The castle itself is sometimes open for guided tours, and you can stop off at The Observatory Science Centre, where astronomy exhibitions illustrate the work and history of the Observatory.

Romans and Normans at Pevensey Levels

DISTANCE 4.5 miles (7.2km)   MINIMUM TIME 1hr 45min

ASCENT/GRADIENT Negligible ▲▲▲   LEVEL OF DIFFICULTY ✦✦✦

PATHS Field paths, brief stretch of road and riverside

LANDSCAPE Low-level former marshland, flat and watery landscape

SUGGESTED MAP AA Walker's Map 30 Eastbourne & Beachy Head

START/FINISH Grid reference: TQ645048

DOG FRIENDLINESS Under control on farmland and minor roads

PARKING Pay-and-display car park by Pevensey Castle

PUBLIC TOILETS At car park

The great harbour here silted up long ago, leaving Pevensey stranded inland, 2 miles (3.2km) from the sea. It was from here that William, Duke of Normandy, marched inland to defeat King Harold and his Saxon army in 1066. What took place represents one of the most significant events in English history.

ROMAN FORTRESS

The exact spot where William came ashore can't be identified, as the coastline has shifted and altered so greatly down the centuries. What is known, however, is that 800 years before the arrival of William, the Romans chose this site to construct the fortress of Anderida as part of their defence of the Saxon Shore. Pevensey was one of a series of fortifications along this coast and the remains of its outer walls survive. Standing up to 30ft (9m) thick in places and enclosing an area of about 10 acres (4ha), the walls are considered to be among the finest examples of Roman building in England.

In 1066, centuries after the Roman invasion of Britain, William, Duke of Normandy, crossed the Channel and came ashore at Pevensey. Determined to claim the English crown, he expected to be met with some resistance at Anderida. But William found the fort undefended, enabling him to consolidate his position immediately. Harold and his men were elsewhere, fighting his brother's Danish army in Yorkshire and expecting William to sail via the Isle of Wight.

The Normans immediately set about erecting one of three prefabricated timber castles they had brought with them, constructing it on a mound of earth within the fort. It was as if they were intent on taking the place of the Romans who had occupied this site so many years before them. Without opposition, the Norman army travelled almost casually through the Sussex countryside, taking food from local

Left: Ruins of Pevensey Castle (Walk 11)

people and burning and looting whatever they could find. Following the Battle of Hastings, William gave the stronghold to his half-brother, Robert, Count of Mortain. It was Robert who built the Norman castle, the remains of which we see today. A keep and bailey were subsequently constructed and in the 13th century a formidable stone curtain wall and gatehouse were added.

FURTHER DEFENCES

Further work took place in the 14th century, but by now the castle was sturdy enough to defend itself and its inhabitants from the strongest opponent. Pevensey was prepared to defend the coast from the threat of Napoleon, and as recently as 1940, pill boxes were installed into the castle walls should German forces invade.

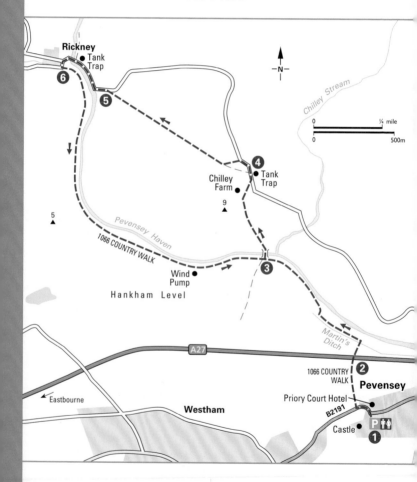

❶ Walk from the car park to the main street, keeping forward on the bend past the castle entrance and the Priory Court Hotel. Pevensey Castle's walls rise up impressively on your left. Bear off to the right just beyond the hotel and a house called The Gables to follow the 1066 Country Walk.

2 Cross the A27 and keep on the trail. Go through a gate and follow the path as it bends left. Continue between fencing and hedging, alongside Martin's Ditch on the left, until you pass through a galvanised gate. Bear right to the riverbank, turn left alongside the Pevensey Haven and saunter past its confluence with the Chilley Stream.

3 Continue for a short distance to a footbridge. Cross over it and then aim diagonally to a footbridge to the right of a house. Carry on across the next field to a stile and footbridge. Bear diagonally right to a wooden gate, then turn right and walk along the track to the road, passing Chilley Farm Shop.

4 Turn left at the lane, and where it bends right go ahead through a gate. Soon reach two gates, and go through the right-hand one. Keep ahead alongside a drainage ditch to a gate in the field corner and continue, keeping the ditch on your left. Make for a footbridge on the left. Cross it and bear right, alongside the ditch.

5 Reach a road, keep left and walk along to the hamlet of Rickney. Avoid the 1066 Country Walk as it runs off to the right and cross the little road bridge. Bear left into Rickney Road at the sign for Hankham and immediately cross a bridge.

6 Turn left after a few paces through a gate and follow the 1066 Country Walk, pass beside a barn to reach a galvanised gate and continue ahead to the right of a pylon along the right-hand field-edge, soon to reach the Pevensey Haven on your left. Continue beside the river. Pass a windpump and the footbridge crossed earlier and then retrace your steps to the A27 and Pevensey.

WHERE TO EAT AND DRINK Chilley Farm Shop serves tea, coffee, ploughman's and a range of tasty sandwiches and cakes. The Royal Oak & Castle Inn and the Smugglers also serve food and coffee, tea and snacks are sold at the castle shop.

WHAT TO SEE The walk passes concrete tank traps, erected in World War II to hinder a German invasion: there are two cylindrical traps by the road near Chilley Farm, and a set of pyramidal ones at Rickney. A former coastal inlet which was drained mainly in the 14th and 15th centuries, the Pevensey Levels have their own individual character. This is a haven for wildlife, plants and insects, as well as home to a great variety of birds, both in summer and winter. Redshank, plovers, snipe and wildfowl visit in winter, while skylarks and kestrels are found here throughout the year.

WHILE YOU'RE THERE Take a stroll through the ancient town of Pevensey and visit the fascinating Court House Museum in the High Street, once the smallest town hall in England. In 1882, under the Municipal Corporation Act, Pevensey lost its status as a borough and in 1890 the Pevensey Town Trust was established to administer the Court House. Inside, you can see the Court Room, Robing Room, cells and exercise yard. There are many exhibits and displays, including a silver penny of William I minted at Pevensey.

Birling Gap to Beachy Head

DISTANCE 7 miles (11.2km) MINIMUM TIME 3hrs

ASCENT/GRADIENT 536ft (163m) ▲▲▲ LEVEL OF DIFFICULTY +++

PATHS Downland paths and tracks, clifftop greensward, no stiles

LANDSCAPE Southern boundary of South Downs and headland

SUGGESTED MAP AA Walker's Map 30 Eastbourne & Beachy Head

START/FINISH Grid reference: TV554959

DOG FRIENDLINESS On lead by Cornish Farm and on South Downs Way

PARKING Pay-and-display National Trust car park at Birling Gap

PUBLIC TOILETS Birling Gap and Beachy Head

The magnificent chalk cliffs of Beachy Head were formed from the shells of billions of minute creatures which fell to the bottom of a subtropical sea. Today, this stretch of coast is one of Britain's most famous landmarks. The treeless South Downs reach the sea in spectacular fashion and over 500ft (152m) below the towering cliffs lies Beachy Head's distinctive red and white lighthouse, standing alone on a remote beach.

DEVIL'S CAPE

The present 142ft (43m) lighthouse, automated in 1983 and modernised in 1999, has been vital to the safety of mariners off this coast since it was completed in 1902. But even as far back as 1670 a beacon shone from this point, helping to guide ships away from the treacherous ledges below. Beachy Head has always been a navigational nightmare. Sailors have long feared it and the Venetians dubbed it the Devil's Cape. In 1831 the eccentric Sussex landowner John Fuller, or 'Mad Jack' as he was known, built the Belle Tout lighthouse high up on the headland to the west of Beachy Head. The lamp was first lit in 1834 but the lighthouse was never a great success. Its lofty position on the cliff top meant that it was often shrouded in mist and fog and therefore invisible to shipping in the English Channel. A decision was eventually taken to erect a lighthouse at sea level.

Everyone has heard of Beachy Head but not many of us know where the name originates. It comes from the Norman French *Beau Chef* – meaning beautiful headland. The description is certainly apt and this breezy, sprawling cliff top draws visitors and tourists from far and wide who come to marvel at the breathtaking sea views or saunter along the South Downs Way. The whole area is a designated Site of Special Scientific Interest (SSSI).

Eastbourne

B2103

B2103

5

SOUTH DOWNS WAY

35

4
155

Beachy Head
Countryside Centre
164

Beachy Head
PH

6

Beachy
Head

Bullockdown
Farm

Beachy
Head
Lighthouse

Frost
Hill

SOUTH DOWNS WAY

Cornish
Farm

3

P

2

Belle Tout
Lighthouse

65

Birling
Gap

1

Birling
Gap
Café

0   ½ mile
0   1km

1 Facing the cottages in the car park, take the leftmost track, by a parking ticket machine near the car park entrance, and parallel to the road. Keep to the right of the next car park and follow the path between the trees.

2 On emerging from the trees, you see a junction with a concrete track on the other side of the road; take the next left path down to meet it. Follow the bridleway signposted 'East Dean Down'. Glance back here for an unexpected view of the old Belle Tout lighthouse. Pass a fingerpost and continue ahead.

3 Follow the concrete track as it bends right towards Cornish Farm, avoiding the faint grass path going straight on. Just before the farm and some pens, go left through a waymarked gate and walk along the spine of the ridge, keeping the fence on your right-hand side. Make for another gate and continue ahead. Pass alongside lines of bushes before reaching the next gate. Down to the right you see Bullockdown Farm, and fields and pastures enclosed by flint walls.

4 Pass beside a barrier to the road and turn right, following the wide grassy verge. On reaching two adjoining barriers and the end of a wall on the right, cross the road and take the grassy path to a five-way junction, bearing half left down a broad grassy track. At the next junction, fork right at the signpost (left is the South Downs Way).

5 100yds (91m) later, turn sharp right on the South Downs Way (ahead is signposted to the Seafront) and follow the long-distance trail as it climbs steadily between bushes and vegetation. Keep right when another path comes in from the left and contour round the slopes, eventually reaching a tarmac path just above an RAF memorial and a viewpoint of Beachy Head lighthouse at the foot of the cliff. Cross the grass, up the slope. In front of you now are the Beachy Head pub and Beachy Head Countryside Centre.

6 Return to the South Downs Way and follow it downhill, with the sea on your left. The path can be seen ahead, running over the undulating cliff top. Keep the Belle Tout lighthouse in your sights and follow the path up towards it. Keep to the right of the old lighthouse and soon the car park at Birling Gap edges into view, as do the famous Seven Sisters cliffs. Carry on down, finally dropping to the right to return to the car park.

WHAT TO SEE By the wooden railings where you first see Beachy Head Lighthouse is a memorial to the 110,000 members of RAF Bomber Command, half of whom died in action. Another 11,000 were taken as prisoners of war. The hill on which Belle Tout Lighthouse stands has a prominent prehistoric ditch running the length of the hill and is thought to be of late Neolithic or early Bronze Age origins.

Right: Along the beach at Birling Gap (Walk 12)

The Snake River and the Seven Sisters

DISTANCE 3 miles (4.8km)	**MINIMUM TIME** 1hr 30min

ASCENT/GRADIENT Negligible ▲▲▲   **LEVEL OF DIFFICULTY** +++

PATHS Grassy trails and well-used paths, mostly beside the Cuckmere or canalised branch of the river

LANDSCAPE Exposed and isolated valley and river mouth

SUGGESTED MAP AA Walker's Map 30 Eastbourne & Beachy Head

START/FINISH Grid reference: TV518995

DOG FRIENDLINESS Under close control within Seven Sisters Country Park. On lead during lambing season and near A259

PARKING Fee-paying car park at Seven Sisters Country Park

PUBLIC TOILETS Opposite car park, by visitor centre

One of the few remaining undeveloped river mouths in the southeast is the gap or cove known as Cuckmere Haven. It is one of the south coast's best-known and most popular beauty spots and was regularly used by smugglers in the 18th century to bring ashore their cargoes of brandy and lace. The Cuckmere River joins the English Channel here, but not before it makes a series of extraordinarily wide loops through lush water-meadows – earning it the occasional epithet 'Snake River'.

Winding ever closer to the sea, the Cuckmere emerges beside the famous white chalk cliffs known as the Seven Sisters. Extending east towards Birling Gap, there are, in fact, eight of these towering chalk faces, with the highest one, Haven Brow (253ft/77m), closest to the river mouth. On the other side of the estuary rise the cliffs of Seaford Head, a nature reserve run by the local authority.

SEVEN SISTERS COUNTRY PARK

The focal point of the lower valley is the Seven Sisters Country Park, an amenity area of 692 acres (280ha) developed by East Sussex County Council. The site is a perfect location for a country park and has been imaginatively planned to blend with the coastal beauty of this fascinating area. There are artificial lakes and park trails, and an old Sussex barn near by has been converted to provide a visitor centre which includes many interesting exhibits and displays.

Wildlife also plays a key role within the park's boundaries, providing naturalists with hours of pleasure and enjoyment. The flowers and insects found here are at their best in early to mid summer, while spring and autumn are a good time to bring your binoculars with you for a close-up view of migrant birds.

Early migrant wheatears are sometimes spotted in the vicinity of the river mouth from late February onwards and are followed later in the season by martins, swallows, whinchats and warblers. Keep a careful eye out for whitethroats, terns and waders too. The lakes and lagoons attract waders such as curlews, sandpipers and little stints. Grey phalaropes have also been seen in the park, usually after severe autumn storms. These elusive birds spend most of their lives far out to sea, usually off South America or western Africa.

The walk explores this very special part of the Cuckmere Valley and begins by heading for the beach. You might wonder why the river meanders the way it does. The meltwaters of the last Ice Age shaped this landscape, and over the centuries rising sea levels and a freshwater peat swamp influenced the river's route to the Channel. Around the start of the 19th century, the sea rose to today's level and a new straight cut with raised banks, devised in 1846, shortened the Cuckmere's journey to the sea. This unnatural waterway controls the river and helps prevent flooding, although in the long term the plan is to allow the valley to revert to salt marsh.

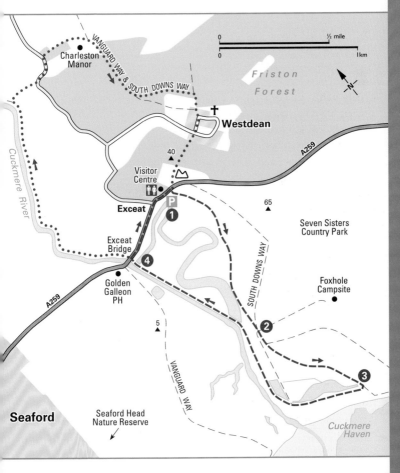

1 From the car park, go through the gate beyond the phone box and the parking ticket machine and follow the wide, grassy path towards the beach. The path gradually curves to the right, merging into a concrete track. The Cuckmere River meanders beside you, heading for the open sea. Continue ahead between the track and the river and make for a South Downs Way sign.

2 Reach a junction with the South Downs Way, avoiding the track to the left over a cattlegrid signposted to Foxhole Campsite. Carry on along through a gate, forking left on the South Downs Way at the next signpost. At the next signpost do not follow the South Downs Way uphill but keep right, signposted to the beach, along low ground with the hillside and fence on your left. Pass a group of wartime pill boxes on the left, an evocative reminder of less peaceful times, and go through a gate. Join a stony path and walk ahead to the beach, with the white wall of the Seven Sisters rearing up beside you.

3 Turn right and cross the shore, approaching an Emergency Point sign; branch off to the right to join another track here. Follow this for about 50yds (46m) until you come to a junction by a line of toothlike concrete wartime tank traps and keep left, following the Park Trail. Keep beside the Cuckmere – the landscape here is characterised by a network of meandering channels and waterways, all feeding into the river. Keep left at the next fork and follow the footpath as it veers left, in line with the Cuckmere. Continue on the straight path by the side of the river.

4 Keep ahead to the road at Exceat Bridge, and on the left is the Golden Galleon pub. Turn right and follow the A259 to return to the car park at the country park.

WHERE TO EAT AND DRINK The Golden Galleon by Exceat Bridge is a very popular 18th-century inn thought to have inspired Rudyard Kipling's poem *Song of the Smugglers*. The menu is traditional and very British. By the visitor centre at the Seven Sisters Country Park is a restaurant and tea rooms, and in summer there is often an ice cream van in the car park.

WHAT TO SEE Shingle plants thrive on the sheltered parts of beaches; a stroll at Cuckmere Haven reveals the yellow horned poppy and the fleshy leaved sea kale. Sea beet, curled dock and scentless chamomile also grow here.

WHILE YOU'RE THERE If you have the time, take a look at the Seaford Head Nature Reserve, which lies on the west side of Cuckmere Haven. This chalk headland, which rises 282ft (85m) above the sea, is a popular local attraction and from here the coastal views are magnificent.

Cuckmere River and Charleston Manor

DISTANCE 5.5 miles (8.8km)   MINIMUM TIME 3hrs

ASCENT/GRADIENT 262ft (80m) ▲▲▲   LEVEL OF DIFFICULTY +++

PATHS Riverside and thick woodland, several stiles

DOG FRIENDLINESS One short stretch of road. Under control in Friston Forest

SEE MAP AND INFORMATION PANEL FOR WALK 13

To make a longer walk in the Cuckmere Valley, cross Exceat Bridge at Point ❹ and continue beside the Cuckmere, following the riverside path through this delightful, though lonely, valley. Swans may be seen gliding on the water. Head for a kissing gate, continue over two stiles and at the marker post with yellow arrows look for a path on the right, just before a stile.

Take the path away from the Cuckmere, following it between trees and bushes. Beyond a gate, keep right as signposted, turn left at the road and pass the entrance to Charleston Manor. Pevsner described Charleston as 'a perfect house in a perfect setting'. Parts of it date from the early 12th century and the house is renowned for its truly splendid gardens and 15th-century double tithe barn.

Immediately after the house, turn right to join a rising enclosed path signposted 'Jevington'. Merge with the Vanguard Way and South Downs Way, joining from the left, and keep right at the next fork, up steps. Follow the South Downs Way signs along the pretty path through Friston Forest. Eventually the power lines leave the path.

Carry on until a signpost points right downhill to the picturesque hamlet of Westdean, lying half-hidden in a wooded hollow. The church dates mostly from the 14th century and the old rectory beside it is probably Norman. Join the road on a bend and continue ahead to a junction. Cross over to a green phone box and walk ahead to a flight of steps alongside a wall.

Make for a stone stile at the top of the steps, where there are glorious views of the Cuckmere River below, winding away towards the sea. This certainly has to be one of the most dramatic and memorable views in all of Sussex. Descend the steep, grassy hillside and make for a kissing gate by the visitor centre. Cross the road and return to the car park.

WHAT TO SEE On the west side of the valley, in view from the river and from Charleston Manor, is a huge carving of a horse known as the Litlington White Horse. The first carving here was created in 1838; the current horse dates from 1924 or 1925.

Alfriston and Berwick

DISTANCE 4 miles (6.4km)	MINIMUM TIME 2hrs

ASCENT/GRADIENT 464ft (141m) ▲▲▲   LEVEL OF DIFFICULTY ✚✚✚

PATHS Exposed paths and tracks

LANDSCAPE Downland to west of Cuckmere Valley

SUGGESTED MAP AA Walker's Map 30 Eastbourne & Beachy Head

START/FINISH Grid reference: TQ520033

DOG FRIENDLINESS Mostly off lead but not permitted at Alfriston Clergy House

PARKING The Willows fee-paying car park, Alfriston

PUBLIC TOILETS Alfriston

With its charming shops, inns and parish church, Alfriston is a classic Sussex village and a key attraction on the tourist trail – posters showing the village fair were used to inspire British troops during World War II.

TIMELESS ALFRISTON

St Andrew's Church is known as the 'Cathedral of the Downs'. Standing on an ancient Anglo-Saxon mound, it is said to mark the spot where four oxen, carrying building materials, lay down to rest.

At the centre of the village is the weathered remains of the market cross. It is one of only two such structures in Sussex (the other being in Chichester) and is thought to date from 1405, when Henry IV granted the village the right to hold a market. A lorry collided with it in 1955, and the shaft is a modern replacement; on top is a carving of a shepherd's crown, a good-luck charm traditionally carried by shepherds.

In centuries past, Alfriston was rife with smuggling activities and harboured one of the most notorious smugglers' gangs. The Market Cross Inn, also known as Ye Olde Smugglers Inne, was once home to Stanton Collins, the gang leader, and reputedly contained numerous secret staircases and hiding holes.

BERWICH CHURCH'S PAINTINGS

From outside this looks like any other country church, but once inside look for the time switch and light up the interior. That way you can appreciate the remarkable wall paintings in all their detail. These murals were commissioned by Bishop Bell of Chichester in 1943 and are the work of Duncan Grant and Vanessa and Quentin Bell, members of the renowned Bloomsbury Group, who lived nearby at Charleston. During World War II many church windows were destroyed by bombs and the Bishop of Chichester considered it more appropriate for artists to decorate church walls rather than design windows. Familiar landmarks were used in the paintings and local people took part as models.

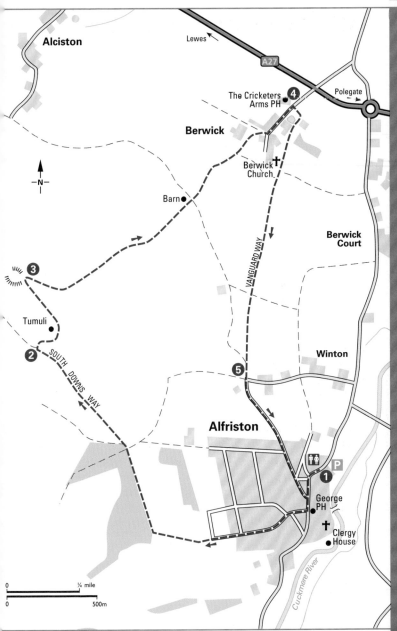

❶ Turn left on leaving the car park and make for the centre of Alfriston. Pass the cross in the main street and turn right by The Star inn, following Star Lane. Go straight over at the junction up King's Ride and continue on the South Downs Way. The road dwindles to a steep flinty track further up. This was originally a drovers' route for sheep being driven to market. Pass two tracks on the right and follow the wide track as it curves gently to the right. This stretch of the walk gives exhilarating views over the Downs and towards Alfriston. Continue on the South Downs Way, forking right at a signpost, then just after cross a track to take a gate ahead. Proceed along a fence and keep going over this high ground.

❷ Turn right through the next gate, signposted Berwick, initially following the path between fences, then bending to the left and dropping steeply. The smooth expanse of Arlington Reservoir is visible in the distance.

❸ 75yds (68m) beyond a gate halfway down the slope, turn sharp right at a junction. Follow the clear path towards the distant spire of Berwick church, joining a hedgerow, and soon forking right at a signpost. Continue along a narrow woodland strip between fields. Join a track near a barn, turn right on it then immediately swing left. Pass a bridleway on the right and continue on the track. Swing right when you

see a sign for farm vehicles and walk along to the Cricketers Arms.

❹ Join the path opposite the pub and follow the Vanguard Way (waymarked VGW). Keep right by the pond, pass beside a house to reach a stile. Cross a field to a gate to Berwick church. Enter the churchyard to view the church. Leave by the same gate, returning to the Vanguard Way by turning right along the field edge, and right again to a gate in the corner. Go straight on at the junction at a point level with the end of the churchyard, following VGW markers. Descend to a gate and follow the waymarked path across open fields, keep forward at the next junction, then climb to join a gravel drive.

❺ Go straight ahead at the junction, avoiding Winton Street on the left. Descend the slope into Alfriston and bear left for the car park, or continue ahead into the village.

WHERE TO EAT AND DRINK The Star at Alfriston has log fires in winter, and serves morning coffee and bar meals. The timbered 14th-century George in the High Street is a cosy place to stop, and has a secluded garden, while the Market Cross (also known as the Smugglers) is a traditional village local. The Singing Kettle, Chestnuts and Badgers Tea House serve morning coffee, light lunches and afternoon tea and are located in the village centre. The Cricketers Arms at Berwick serves traditional home-made food, with the emphasis on local produce, meat and fish.

WHAT TO SEE On the edge of the green at Alfriston is an old mine, washed up on the Cuckmere River in October 1943 and rendered inactive by the naval authorities in World War II. Read the notice which invites you to spare a coin – 'in grateful thanks that Alfriston is not just another ruin which would have been the case had the mine exploded'.

WHILE YOU'RE THERE Visit the National Trust's Clergy House at Alfriston. This oak-framed, thatched building dates back to about 1350 and was built to cater for a number of confined parish priests in the aftermath of the Black Death. The National Trust acquired the Clergy House as their very first property in 1896, paying just £10.

Wilmington's Long Man

DISTANCE 6.25 miles (10km)   MINIMUM TIME 2hrs 30min

ASCENT/GRADIENT 465ft (142m) ▲▲▲   LEVEL OF DIFFICULTY ✦✦✦

PATHS Downland paths and tracks, stretch of country road

LANDSCAPE Dramatic downland on east side of Cuckmere Valley

SUGGESTED MAP AA Walker's Map 30 Eastbourne & Beachy Head

START/FINISH Grid reference: IQ543042

DOG FRIENDLINESS Some enclosed tracks suitable for dogs off lead

PARKING Free long-stay car park at Wilmington

PUBLIC TOILETS At car park

One of Britain's most impressive and enduring mysteries is the focal point of this highly scenic walk high on the Downs. Cut into the turf below Windover Hill, the chalk figure of the Long Man of Wilmington is the largest representation of the human figure in western Europe, and yet it remains an enigma, its origins shrouded in mystery. For centuries experts have been trying to solve this ancient puzzle but no one has been able to prove conclusively who he is or what he symbolises.

HELMETED WAR-GOD

For many years the earliest record of the Long Man was thought to have been a drawing by the antiquarian William Burrell, made when he visited Wilmington Priory in 1766. Then, in 1993, a new drawing was discovered, made by John Rowley, a surveyor, as long ago as 1710. Though the new drawing has confirmed some theories, it has not been able to shed any real light as to the Long Man's true identity or why this particular hillside was chosen. However, it does suggest that the original figure was a shadow or indentation in the grass rather than a bold line. It seems there were distinguishing facial features which may have long faded; the staves being held were not a rake and a scythe as once described and the head was originally a helmet shape, indicating that the Long Man may have been a helmeted war-god.

Until the 19th century the chalk figure was only visible in a certain light, particularly when there was a dusting of snow or frost on the ground. In 1874, a public subscription was raised through *The Times* and the figure re-cut. To help define the outline of the Long Man, the site was marked out in yellow bricks, though this may have resulted in the feet being incorrectly positioned.

CAMOUFLAGED

In 1925 the Long Man of Wilmington was given to the Sussex Archaeological Trust, which later became the Sussex Archaeological

Society. During World War II the site was camouflaged to prevent enemy aircraft from using it as a landmark. In 1969 further restoration work began, and the yellow bricks were replaced with pre-cast concrete blocks. These are frequently painted now, so that the shape of the Long Man stands out from a considerable distance.

Photographed from the air, the figure is elongated, but when viewed from ground level an optical illusion is created and he assumes normal human proportions. Do this walk on a cold winter's day and the Long Man's ghostly aura, and the remoteness of the surroundings, will be enough to send a shiver down the spine.

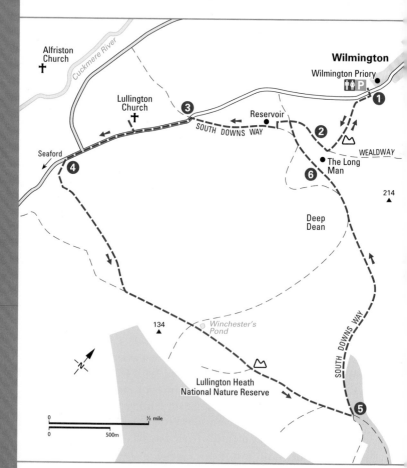

1 Make for the car park exit, cross the road and turn right to follow the path parallel to the road, heading towards the Long Man of Wilmington. Bear left at the barrier and take the Wealdway to the chalk figure. Climb quite steeply, curving to the right. Go through a gate and go straight ahead towards the escarpment, veering right just below the figure of the Long Man.

2 Go through the next gate, cross a track and bear left as soon as a fenced-covered reservoir comes into view ahead. A few paces brings you to a gate and a sign for the South Downs Way. Turn right on a track and pass the reservoir.

3 Turn left on the road and walk down to a signpost by two wooden garages for Lullington church, following the path alongside several cottages. After visiting the church, retrace your steps to the road and turn right. Head down the lane and past a turning for Alfriston on the right, and continue ahead towards Seaford.

4 Just after a postbox, turn left on a rising track, signposted 'Jevington'. Follow this as it climbs steadily between tracts of remote downland. Keep left at the next main junction, then at the second junction by a small flint pillar keep forward, past the entrance gate to Winchester's Pond on your left. Lullington Heath National Nature Reserve is on the right now. At the bottom of a dip, continue forward (ignoring a track to the right) and keep on the track as it climbs steeply. Pass a second sign.

5 Where the trees begin, reach a junction with the South Downs Way and turn left to follow the enclosed path to a gate. Go straight ahead slightly above the woodland and pass through a wooden gate. The path begins a gradual curve to the left and eventually passes along the rim of a spectacular dry valley known as Deep Dean. Keep the fence on your left and look for a gate ahead. Swing right as you approach it to a stile and then follow the path alongside the fence, crossing along the top of the Long Man.

6 Glance to your right and you can just make out the head and body of the chalk figure down below. It's an intriguing view. Continue keeping the fence on the right, avoiding joining the main track which bends left towards the reservoir, and descend to a gate. Turn right here and retrace your steps to the car park at Wilmington.

WHERE TO EAT AND DRINK At the far end of the car park is a pleasant picnic area. The Giant's Rest in Wilmington is a popular pub at the northern end of the village. Alternatively, by the A27 is the Wishing Well Tea Rooms, serving home-made soups, sandwiches and cakes.

WHAT TO SEE Wilmington Priory was founded for the Benedictine abbey of Grestain in Normandy, and much of the present building dates from the 14th century. As few as two or three monks resided here, and they used the parish church in Wilmington rather than build their own place of worship. The monks were engaged in managing the abbey's English estates. The priory is in the care of the Landmark Trust and used as a holiday let, so not open to the public. Only 16ft (5m) square, 13th-century Lullington church stands above the Cuckmere valley and is one of Britain's smallest churches.

WHILE YOU'RE THERE Make a detour to look at the Lullington Heath National Nature Reserve, which consists of scrubland, chalk grassland and the best example of chalk heath still surviving in Britain. Various heathers and orchids also grow here. Study the maps displayed along the reserve boundary to help you follow the reserve's paths and bridleways.

Arlington's Lakeside Trail

DISTANCE 3 miles (4.8km)	MINIMUM TIME 1hr 30min	
ASCENT/GRADIENT 82ft (25m) ▲▲▲	LEVEL OF DIFFICULTY +++	

PATHS Field paths and trail, some brief road walking, many stiles

LANDSCAPE Level lakeside terrain and gentle farmland

SUGGESTED MAP AA Walker's Map 30 Eastbourne & Beachy Head

START/FINISH Grid reference: TQ528074

DOG FRIENDLINESS Mostly on lead, as requested by signs on route

PARKING Fee-paying car park at Arlington Reservoir

PUBLIC TOILETS At car park

It was in 1971 that Arlington's rural landscape changed irrevocably in both character and identity. A vital new reservoir was opened, supplying water to the nearby communities of Eastbourne, Hailsham, Polegate and Heathfield. Study the informative blurb on the grassy bank and you'll learn that the area of the reservoir is equivalent to 121 football pitches and that the maximum depth of the lake is 37ft (11.3m), deep enough to submerge four single-decker buses.

The 120-acre (46ha) reservoir was formed by cleverly cutting off a meander in the Cuckmere River and it's now an established site for wintering wildfowl, as well as home to a successful rainbow trout fishery. Besides the trout, bream, perch, roach and eels make up Arlington's underwater population. Fly fishing is a popular activity here and the lake draws anglers from all over Sussex.

The local nature reserve was originally planted with more than 30,000 native trees, including oak, birch, wild cherry, hazel and hawthorn. The grassland areas along the shoreline are intentionally left uncut to enable many kinds of moth and butterfly to thrive in their natural habitats. Orchids grow here too.

BIRD WATCHING

Arlington Reservoir, a designated Site of Special Scientific Interest (SSSI), is a favourite haunt of many birds on spring and autumn migrations and up to 10,000 wildfowl spend their winter here, including large numbers of mallard and wigeon. The shoveler duck is also a frequent visitor and most common as a bird of passage. You can identify the head of the shoveler drake by its dark, bottle-green colouring and broad bill. The breast is white and the underparts bright chestnut, while its brown and black back has a noticeable blue sheen. The female duck is mottled brown.

Great crested grebes, Canada geese and nightingales are also known to inhabit the reservoir area, making Arlington a popular destination for ornithologists. See if you can spot the blue flash of a kingfisher on the water; its colouring so distinctive it would be hard to confuse it with any other bird. It's also known for its piercing whistles as it swoops low over the water. The reservoir and its environs are home to fallow deer and foxes, so keep a sharp look-out as you walk around the lake.

The walk begins in the main car park by the reservoir, though initially views of the lake are obscured by undergrowth and a curtain of trees. After visiting the village of Arlington, where there is a welcome pub, the return leg is directly beside the water, providing a constantly changing scenic backdrop to round off the walk.

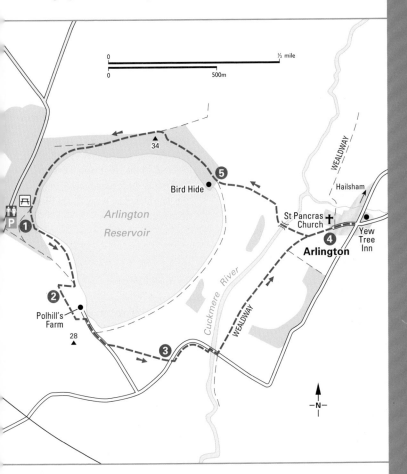

① From the car park walk towards the information board and map. Turn right on the circular walk by the reservoir, soon passing a small picnic area, and ignoring a fork to the right. Carry on until eventually the path reaches a driveway, with a gate to the left signed 'No entry – farm access only'; here cross over following the footpath and bridleway signs.

2 Skirt the buildings of Polhill's Farm and return to walk along the tarmac lane. Turn right and walk along to a kissing gate and a 'circular walk' sign. Ignore the gate and keep on the lane. Continue for about 50 yards (46m) and then branch left over a stile into a field. Swing half right and look for a second stile to the right of an overgrown pond. Cross a third stile and go across a pasture to a fourth stile.

3 Cross the road and turn left to follow the path parallel with the road. Rejoin the road, cross the Cuckmere River and then bear left to join the Wealdway, following the sign for Arlington. Walk along the drive and when it curves to the right, by some houses, veer left over a stile. Head for the spire of Arlington church, keeping ahead when you reach the right-hand fence corner and following the waymark. Cross another stile and a wooden footbridge. Keep to the right of the church, cross another stile and walk along the lane to the Yew Tree Inn.

4 From the pub, retrace your steps to the church and cross over the field to the footbridge. Turn right immediately beyond it to a stile in the field corner. Cross the pasture to the prominent metal footbridge over the Cuckmere and continue to cross over a plank bridge, then head across the field towards a line of trees, following the vague outline of a path. The reservoir's embankment is clearly defined on the left as you begin a gentle ascent.

5 Cross a stile by a galvanised gate and go through a kissing gate on the immediate right. Follow the path alongside the lake and pass a bird hide on the left. Keep left further on and keep to the bridleway as it reveals glimpses of the lake through the trees. Veer left at the fork and then follow the path alongside the reservoir back to the car park.

WHERE TO EAT AND DRINK Arlington Reservoir has a picnic site by the car park where you can relax before or after the walk. The Yew Tree Inn at Arlington has a children's play area, beer garden and a choice of home-cooked dishes. Lunch and dinner are served every day and there is a choice of real ales. Nearby are the Arlington Tea Rooms and the Old Oak Inn, originally the village almshouse and dating from 1733.

WHAT TO SEE Call into Arlington's St Pancras Church. It has Saxon origins, as seen in its 'long and short work' outside, and fragments of wall paintings inside, as well as an impressive timber roof with huge kingposts and trusses.

WHILE YOU'RE THERE Stop off at the Arlington bird hide and see if you can identify members of Arlington's feathered population. In spring you might spot an osprey, a large bird which occasionally visits lakes, fens and estuaries and preys almost exclusively on fish. Look out too for house martins, sand martins, sandpipers, blackcaps, kestrels, mallards and dunlins – among other birds.

Downland Views Over Firle

DISTANCE 4.25 miles (6.8km)	MINIMUM TIME 2hrs

ASCENT/GRADIENT 476ft (145m) ▲▲▲   LEVEL OF DIFFICULTY ✛✛✛

PATHS Tracks, paths and roads

LANDSCAPE Downland and farmland

SUGGESTED MAP AA Walker's Map 30 Eastbourne & Beachy Head

START/FINISH Grid reference: TQ468075

DOG FRIENDLINESS On lead in vicinity of Firle Place and near livestock

PARKING Free car park in Firle

PUBLIC TOILETS Firle Place and Charleston Farmhouse

Stroll along the South Downs Way between Alfriston and the River Ouse and you can look down towards the sleepy village of Firle, nestling amid a patchwork of fields and hedgerows below the escarpment. There is something that sets this place apart from most other communities. Firle is an estate village with a tangible feudal atmosphere.

FIRLE PLACE: A PALLADIAN MANSION

At the centre of the village lies Firle Place, home to the Gage family for over 500 years and now open to the public. The 18th-century house is magnificent, though it hardly looks classically English. It's built of a pale Caen stone from Normandy that may have been recycled from St Pancras Priory in Lewes, with a hipped roof, dormers and a splendid Venetian window surmounting the rusticated central archway in the east front.

Firle Place is surrounded by sweeping parkland and set against a magnificent backdrop of hanging woods. The name is Old English and means 'oak'. No house could occupy a finer location. A tour of the house reveals some fascinating treasures, many of which were brought back from America by Sir Thomas, 1st Viscount Gage. The paintings include an important collection of Old Masters with works by Van Dyck, Reynolds, Gainsborough and Rubens, and there are also collections of Sèvres porcelain and English and French furniture.

A PLACE IN HISTORY

The present Palladian mansion conceals part of an older Tudor building. This was later enlarged by Sir John Gage, Vice Chamberlain and Captain of the Royal Guard in the court of Henry VIII. In 1542, when James V of Scotland was killed at Solway Moss, he commanded the King's troops against the Scottish army. He also superintended the executions of Queen Catherine Howard and Lady Jane Grey while Constable of the Tower of London. Sir Edward, his son, as Sheriff of Sussex, was responsible for ensuring that the Lewes Martyrs were burned, but the family later converted to the Roman Catholic faith and were forced to retire from public life. Later, the horticulturalist Thomas Gage introduced the Reine Claude plum to Britain – it became known as the greengage.

Little remains of the external features of the original courtyard house. The house underwent major changes in 1745, remodelled by Sir William Gage. He and his cousin and successor, Sir Thomas, rebuilt the house in Palladian manner with many rococo elaborate features. Another famous family member, General Thomas Gage, was Commander-in-Chief of the British forces at the beginning of the American War of Independence.

Firle is a perfect example of what landscape historians describe as a 'closed village'. Such settlements, growing up on private estates, enjoy a unique status and are a vivid reminder of the autocracy of generations of

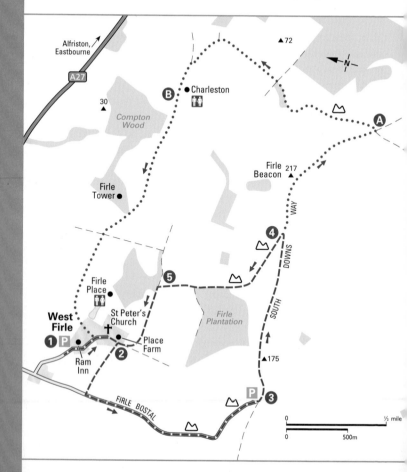

powerful land-owning families. The development of Firle was severely regulated and it was virtually impossible for outsiders to move into the village, which has for many years provided important employment and accommodation, operating as a self-contained community.

1 Turn left out of the car park, pass the Ram Inn and follow the road round to the right, through the village of Firle. Walk past the village stores. Pass the turning to Firle's Church of St Peter and continue heading southwards, out of the village.

2 Past Place Farm and its forge, turn right at a junction of concrete tracks and carry on until a T-junction, where you turn left up the road; the climb is steep in places. At the top, turn left through the car park, swing left to a gate and join the South Downs Way.

3 Head eastwards on the long-distance trail, later passing a square concrete tank.

4 When you reach a blue-arrowed marker post turn sharp left, initially along the top but soon heading down the steep slopes of the escarpment. Keep descending all the way, as the path veers right. Drop down to reach a gate and walk ahead, keeping a fence on the left. Skirt around Firle Plantation and follow the track all the way to the junction.

5 Bear left and walk along the track, alongside the estate wall on your right, keeping the dramatic escarpment on the left. As you approach the village of Firle, the track curves to the right towards the buildings of Place Farm. Cross over the junction of concrete tracks and retrace your steps back to the car park at the other end of the village.

WHERE TO EAT AND DRINK Try the Ram Inn at Firle.

WHAT TO SEE In Firle's main street is the quaint old village stores. Up until motor cars began to make shopping in towns and cities easier, Firle benefited from a tailor, a bootmaker, a butcher and a baker. A blacksmith, a miller and a harness maker also operated in the village.

WHILE YOU'RE THERE It's always pleasing to find a church open to visitors, and many in Sussex keep their doors unlocked throughout the year. Firle church is no exception and the sign at the entrance states that the door is open from dawn to dusk. The parish refuses 'to be deterred by occasional thefts, believing it must be available to the people of the village'. There is a fee for brass rubbing, which should be paid at the village stores. The church includes a window dedicated to Henry Rainald Gage KCVO, the 6th Viscount, who succeeded to the title in his 17th year in 1912 and died in 1982. The window depicting a ram and the South Downs was designed by the late John Piper and is possibly his last work in stained glass.

Firle Beacon and Charleston

DISTANCE 6 miles (9.7km) **MINIMUM TIME** 3hrs 30min

ASCENT/GRADIENT 576ft (175m) ▲▲▲ **LEVEL OF DIFFICULTY** +++

SEE MAP AND INFORMATION PANEL FOR WALK 18

To extend Walk 18 don't turn sharp left at Point **4**. Instead, continue along the South Downs Way to Firle Beacon, passing a trig point. Look out for a bridleway crossing over the South Downs Way and bear left at Point **A**. Make for a gate and head diagonally down the downland escarpment.

Aim for a gate and skirt a belt of woodland before continuing straight on at a junction of tracks. Pass a house called Tilton Meadow and bear left at the next junction, by some barns. Follow the concrete bridleway past a right-angled bend, then immediately after turn left towards Charleston, Point **B**, once the home of Duncan Grant and Clive and Vanessa Bell, members of the Bloomsbury Set. If you have time, visit the house; it includes examples of decorated furniture and murals. Look for home-made details such as the beaded lampshades, upturned pottery colanders, or a woolly fringe concealing a radiator. The walled garden is a mass of cottage planting and dense colour.

Keep ahead through gates along the track, then forward along the left edge of a field. Go through the gate on the left at the far corner then turn right to resume the same direction, up across fields and just below Firle Tower. This Gothic eye-catcher was built in 1819 to accommodate the estate gamekeeper.

Cross a track, pass through trees and enter a field. Firle Place, in its lovely downland setting, can be seen from this spot. Keep to the right-hand edge of the field, and almost immediately bear diagonally left towards some houses. Join a wall and go through the gap at the wall corner. Go through a wrought-iron gate by the right-hand side of the houses and cross the rough lane to a footpath and gate. Follow the waymarked path across the parkland, cross the main drive just to the right of the signpost to Firle Place, and follow a track to the gate. Continue beyond it on a track and follow it to the road. Turn right and return to the car park at Firle.

WHERE TO EAT AND DRINK The Ram Inn at Firle serves imaginative food and is a fine example of a traditional, old-style village pub. The Ram is open all day. Firle Place has a licensed restaurant serving lunches and cream teas. There is a tea terrace offering delightful views over the gardens. The cafe at Charleston serves tasty salads and sandwiches.

By the Bluebell Railway at Horsted Keynes

DISTANCE 5 miles (8km)　MINIMUM TIME 2hrs

ASCENT/GRADIENT 230ft (70m) ▲▲▲　LEVEL OF DIFFICULTY ✚✚✚

PATHS Field and woodland paths and tracks, quiet roads, several stiles

LANDSCAPE Peaceful woodland and farmland with views

SUGGESTED MAP AA Leisure Map 23 Brighton & The South Downs

START/FINISH Grid reference: TQ385282

DOG FRIENDLINESS Off lead on parts of West Sussex Border Path (not allowed in ponds). Under control in vicinity of Horsted Keynes and railway station

PARKING Horsted Keynes rural car park (free) by Horsted Club in village centre

PUBLIC TOILETS Horsted Keynes station (seasonal opening) and village

Many of us become instantly nostalgic when we think about the great days of the steam railways. There is something wonderfully evocative about the sound of an approaching steam train. Even standing on the platform of an authentically restored station and gazing fondly at the livery, the bookstalls and the adverts for seaside holidays can rekindle a host of cherished memories.

Horsted Keynes station is just such a place, a railway enthusiast's dream come true. The station lies on the famous Bluebell Railway, a popular attraction since it came in to private ownership in 1960, with a section of line reopening within two years of its closure by British Rail. Volunteers and dedicated members of its preservation society have played a crucial role in establishing, restoring and maintaining the railway. Being the first heritage railway to open in Britain, it managed to obtain an impressive amount of railway-related items, including some wonderful period carriages that include a 1913 observation car, locomotives, old signs and station furnishings. There is also a viewing gallery for the workshop where carriages are restored.

The intention is to recreate a sleepy Sussex junction in the years before World War II. Although essentially a museum recalling the heyday of steam travel, the station really does have the feel of that period. It's like stepping into a time warp, the calendar forever stopped at 1925. Over the years the railway has featured in several television adverts, dramas and films, including the films *Room with a View* and *Miss Potter*, as well as appearing as Downton station in the TV series *Downton Abbey*. The other stations on the line also have an enchanting period setting: Kingscote evokes the 1950s, while Sheffield Park, with its old station lamps and vintage enamel advertisements, recreates a country railway station of the 1880s.

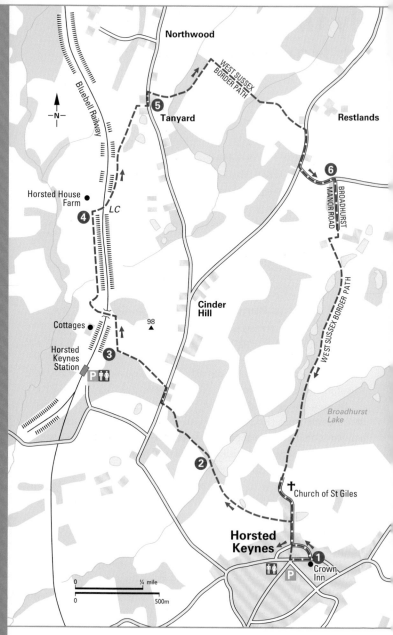

Northwood

WEST SUSSEX BORDER PATH

Bluebell Railway

—N—

5 Tanyard

Restlands

Horsted House Farm

LC

4

BROADHURST

MANOR ROAD

6

Cinder Hill

Cottages

98 ▲

Horsted Keynes Station

P 🚻

3

WEST SUSSEX BORDER PATH

Broadhurst Lake

2

✝ Church of St Giles

Horsted Keynes

P

🚻

1

Crown Inn

0   ¼ mile

0   500m

1 Opposite the village sign by the Crown Inn, go down Church Lane, bearing right downhill at the next junction and turning left immediately beyond a tile-hung cottage called Timbers, on a path between fences. Go through a gate and into the trees, past a pond. Beyond a kissing gate, reach a junction with a track and continue ahead up a path that immediately drops to a junction by a signpost. Go straight over past an angling club sign and pass along the left side of a lake.

② Just after a weir keep left at the fork, over plank footbridges. Carry on in this direction past a public footpath sign, emerge into a field and carry on to reach a road. Turn right on the road for 80yds (73m), then go left opposite a house on a signposted path between fences, skirting paddocks. Emerge on grass above Horsted Keynes station, and turn left to look at the station.

③ With the station on your left, walk up the track, keeping the railway line on your left. Just after the track veers left, cross the footbridge, turning right on the opposite side of the track. Follow the path as it heads away from the Bluebell Railway and crosses two stiles before quickly returning to the line. Turn left and walk alongside it.

④ At a footpath sign, cross the track to a stile, now keeping the railway on your left. Go over a minor lane (which goes over a bridge to your left), and keep alongside the right-hand edge of two fields to a kissing gate. Follow the path across the pasture to the next stile and follow the path beyond.

⑤ Turn left on the road for about 60yds (54m) to a signposted gate on the right. Follow the path down the field and into some woodland, crossing a narrow walkway (care needed) along the rim of a pond. Turn left on the other side, up through the trees to a field, turn left and follow the path right around the field-edge and down to a gap in the vegetation and trees. Descend to a footbridge and go up to a kissing gate and field. Bear left and skirt the pasture to a stile and gate. Exit to the road, turn right along it, then left at the next junction into Broadhurst Manor Road.

⑥ Bear right at the West Sussex Border Path sign and walk along to the entrance to Broadhurst Manor. Veer right at the pond, still on the waymarked trail, which bends left, and follow the signposted track past a series of ponds to Broadhurst Lake on the left. Continue into Church Lane to reach the Church of St Giles. When the lane veers right into Leighton Road, go straight on to return to Horsted Keynes village centre and the green.

WHERE TO EAT AND DRINK There is an excellent picnic area for fine summer days and and cafe at Horsted Keynes station. In Horsted Keynes, the Crown Inn is a stone-built pub on the village green, facing the Green Man; both serve food.

WHAT TO SEE The lovely old Church of St Giles at Horsted Keynes is worth a look. To the right of the entrance lie the graves of former Conservative prime minister Harold Macmillan, his wife Dorothy and their son Maurice. The Macmillans lived at nearby Birch Grove.

WHILE YOU'RE THERE Make a day of it by taking a trip on the Bluebell Railway before the walk or after it. One of the most popular destinations on the line is Sheffield Park, famous for its beautiful 120-acre (49ha) garden which is situated close to the station. The garden was created with the help of 'Capability' Brown and is noted for its spring flowering rhododendrons and dazzling autumn colours.

Overleaf: View over gentle hills and fields at Ashdown Forest (Walk 21)

Winnie-the-Pooh's Ashdown Forest

DISTANCE 7 miles (11.3km)   MINIMUM TIME 3hrs 30min

ASCENT/GRADIENT 170ft (52m) ▲▲▲   LEVEL OF DIFFICULTY ✦✦✦

PATHS Paths and tracks across farmland and woodland, many stiles

LANDSCAPE Undulating farmland and dense woodland

SUGGESTED MAP AA Leisure Map 23 Brighton & The South Downs

START/FINISH Grid reference: TQ473332

DOG FRIENDLINESS Some woodland stretches suitable for dogs off lead.
On lead where notices indicate

PARKING Pooh car park (free), off B2026 south of Hartfield

PUBLIC TOILETS None on route

NOTES Five Hundred Acre Wood is privately owned – keep to the Wealdway

If as a child you were spellbound by the magic of *Winnie-the-Pooh*, then this enjoyable woodland walk will rekindle many happy memories of AA Milne's wonderful stories. The walk skirts Ashdown Forest, the real-life setting for *Winnie-the-Pooh*; it represents the largest area of uncultivated land in southeast England, covering about 20 square miles (58sq km) in northern East and West Sussex. Once part of the much larger Wealden Forest, the area is now a very attractive mix of high, open heathland and oak and birch woodland scattered across the well-wooded sandstone hills of the High Weald.

WILD BEAUTY

Ashdown was a royal forest for 300 years, established by John of Gaunt in 1372. Then, it was a place of wild beauty and thick woodland, so dense in places that at one time over a dozen guides were required to lead travellers from one end to the other. After the Restoration of Charles II in 1660, large parts of the forest were enclosed and given to Royalist supporters. About 6,400 acres (2,500ha) were dedicated to the Commoners and remain freely accessible to the public. Ashdown Forest today is the domain of the city dweller seeking peaceful recreation in the country. Despite this, it is still largely unspoilt.

There is much more to this place than trees. At first glance, the forest's vegetation may look rather uniform but closer inspection reveals considerable variation. In the valley bottoms, wet bogs proliferate, dominated by sphagnum mosses. Round-leaved sundew, marsh clubmoss and cottongrass also thrive in many of the bogs. The distinctive deep blue flowers of marsh gentians add a dash of colour during the autumn. The open pools are home to the nymphs of dragonflies and damselflies while the drier valley slopes are carpeted with plants such as ling, bell heather and bracken. The higher ground supports gorse and purple moor-grass.

The walk begins in a corner of (privately owned) Five Hundred Acre Wood – the 'Hundred Acre Wood' of AA Milne's stories. The return leg briefly follows a disused railway line before heading south, passing close to Cotchford Farm (where AA Milne lived), and crossing Pooh Bridge, built in 1907 and restored in 1979. This is where Milne portrays Winnie-the- Pooh and Christopher Robin playing 'Poohsticks'.

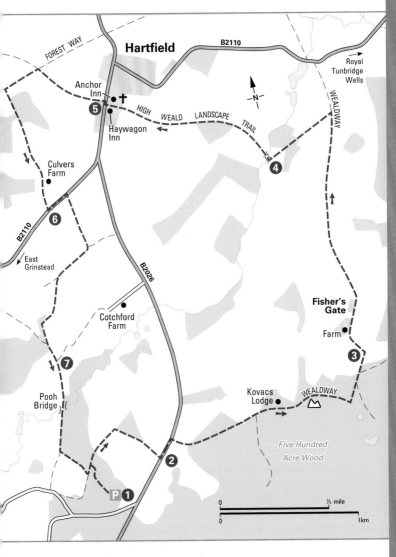

❶ Follow the path through the gate at the bottom of the car park, signed 'Pooh Bridge', and just after a path joins from the left, fork right over a plank bridge to enter a field. Go forward along the left-hand field-edge to a track in the corner; turn right. Cross a drive to a stile and keep ahead, following the path around a paddock to a stile and the road.

2 Turn left onto the road, bear right opposite The Paddocks and follow the path through Five Hundred Acre Wood, dropping to cross a stream by a footbridge away to the left to reach the Wealdway. Continue ahead, following WW markers, passing Kovacs Lodge. Follow further WW markers, keeping left at a junction, then just after a house called Forest Place bear left to leave the forest. Take the path to the right of two gates, below the sign for 'Fisher's Gate'.

3 Follow the path parallel to the drive to skirt the house. Rejoin the drive and keep right, following the Wealdway as it cuts across undulating farmland for 0.75 miles (1.2km). Pass a turning to Old Buckhurst and then bear left over a stile to follow the High Weald Landscape Trail. Cross the field past a clump of trees to enter woodland. Follow the woodland track, soon forking right.

4 Turn right over a brick bridge at the far side of the wood and follow the fence, passing a house. Go through the gateway in the field corner and make for the field ahead. Head diagonally left across farmland to a stile. Keep to the right edge of the field to a stile, then cross a footbridge and continue by the field-edge towards the church. Turn left at a stile and enter the village of Hartfield.

5 Bear right at the B2026, then immediately left along the left-hand edge of a recreation ground. Cross a stile in the field corner and continue over the next stile to the Forest Way. Turn left and follow the old railway trackbed, forking left to a gate just before the trackbed crosses a bridge. Cross the pasture to a gate and follow the woodland bridleway. Emerging from the trees, continue to Culvers Farm.

6 Turn left on the road and walk along to the first right-hand footpath, signposted 'Pooh Bridge'. Take the track ahead, soon passing a wooden shelter and, after going through woodland, emerge by fields and turn right on an enclosed path past a white house. Cross a drive to another stile and head diagonally down the field to a stile in the corner. Continue on the path and head for the next stile, then follow the lane ahead and slightly to the left.

7 After 80yds (73m), fork right by a signpost, go straight on along the public bridleway to Pooh Bridge, and follow the track all the way to Pooh car park, avoiding minor side turnings.

WHERE TO EAT AND DRINK There is a popular tea room in the Pooh Corner Shop, and, on the route of the walk in the village centre, are the Anchor Inn and Haywaggon Inn; both serve food.

WHAT TO SEE Approaching the village of Hartfield, note the 700-year-old church and its ancient lychgate which includes a good example of pargeting or ornamental plasterwork. Picturesque Lych Gate Cottage is one of the oldest and smallest houses in the area. Try to find the plaque indicating an approximate date of 1520. Nearby is an ancient yew tree, often found in country churchyards. The yew is thought to be a symbol of mortality and resurrection, providing protection from evil.

Classic Cuckfield

DISTANCE 5 miles (8km)   MINIMUM TIME 2hrs 30min

ASCENT/GRADIENT 230ft (70m) ▲▲▲   LEVEL OF DIFFICULTY +++

PATHS Field, woodland and parkland paths, minor roads

LANDSCAPE Rolling farmland, attractive parkland and woodland

SUGGESTED MAP AA Leisure Map 23 Brighton & The South Downs

START/FINISH Grid reference: TQ304246

DOG FRIENDLINESS Enclosed paths and tracks suitable for dogs off lead.
On lead on farmland and busy roads

PARKING Free car park in Broad Street, Cuckfield

PUBLIC TOILETS At car park

Standing 400ft (122m) above sea level, in the shadow of Haywards Heath, Cuckfield is one of those fortunate places that has largely escaped the threat of urban development, retaining its charm and character. It is generally thought of as a village and yet it has the feel of a classic country town that has stayed small and compact – something of a rarity in Sussex these days. It was the determination of the Sergison family back in the 19th century not to allow a railway to run across their land that saved Cuckfield from becoming yet another commuter town. The line was diverted to the east and provided the impetus for Haywards Heath instead.

CUCKOO'S CLEARING

Following the Norman Conquest, Cuckfield was held by the Earls Warenne and was granted a charter in 1254. The pronunciation, 'Cookfield', unusual in southern England, stems from its meaning, the delightful 'cuckoo-field'. *The Clearing where the Cuckoo Came* is also the title of a book of poetry about the village.

There are many notable buildings in the High Street and South Street, distinguished by a variety of architectural styles, but it is the famous tower and tall spire of the 15th-century Church of Holy Trinity that stands head and shoulders above the rooftops of Cuckfield. From here you can look towards the Clayton Windmills, known as Jack and Jill, high up on the South Downs.

The church, which has an unusually large churchyard, evolved from a chapel in the 13th and 14th centuries and was restored in the mid-1850s. There are various memorials and brasses inside; but the one feature which never fails to impress is the unique ceiling which boasts a 15th-century framework with moulded bosses. It is thought to have been the gift of the grandson of John of Gaunt who lived in Cuckfield in 1464. It was adorned with painted panels by a local artist in 1865.

Outside in the churchyard, by the Church Street lychgate, is a memorial 'in proud and grateful memory of those men of the 2nd Battalion Post Office Rifles who were billeted and trained in Cuckfield between November 1914 and May 1915 before joining the battalion in France and who never returned'. A stone's throw from the church lies Ockenden Manor, now a hotel. The name is Old English, meaning 'Occa's woodland pasture', and for several centuries it was owned by the Burrell family who improved and extended the building.

The walk begins in the centre of Cuckfield and after passing through the churchyard, with its views of the South Downs, heads southeast, then west across country to the little village of Ansty. A narrow lane leads north to Cuckfield Park, its open parkland enhancing this very attractive walk.

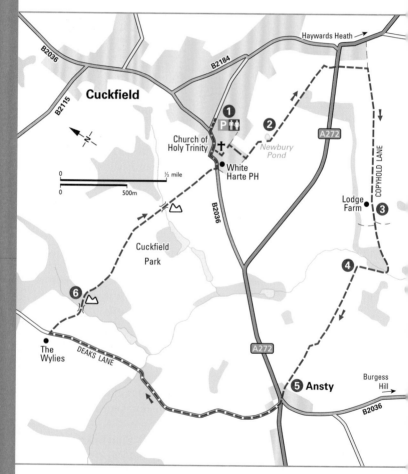

❶ Leave the car park by turning left into Broad Street. Bear left again at the mini-roundabout and walk down to turn left into Church Street. Make for the lychgate by the parish church and enter the churchyard. Head for a kissing gate on the far side, turn left and follow the track.

2 Pass Newbury Pond and cross a stile. Keep ahead along the field boundary on the left, before crossing a stile to join a path running inside the top edge of woodland. Reach a signposted junction in front of some houses and turn right. Follow the path down to the busy A272, cross over to a stile and follow the path through the trees. Turn right on reaching Copyhold Lane, later ignoring a left fork to Copyhold House.

3 Pass Lodge Farm and, when the lane swings round to the left, go straight on at the public bridleway sign, ignoring the path on the right by Copyhold Cottage. Follow the woodland path down to a lane. Go straight on, cross over a stream and immediately turn right to join a footpath, soon crossing a footbridge. Once in the field, keep to the right field-edge.

4 At the field corner turn left by a signpost (avoiding the stile) following the field boundary, and enter the next field via a gap in the hedge. At the end of this large field reach a footpath sign on the bend of a track. Keep ahead, passing a house on the right, and soon reach the A272 at Ansty.

5 Cross over and follow Bolney Road, turning right into Deaks Lane. Pass Ansty Farm and head out of the village. Keep to the lane for over a mile (1.6km) and, just after Cuckfield Cattery and a pond on the right, turn right opposite a house called The Wylies. Pass through a gate and follow the High Weald Landscape Trail down the field.

6 Cross a stile and footbridge and climb steeply through the woodland, soon proceeding between fences. Leave the woodland by a kissing-gate: this is the edge of Cuckfield Park. Cross a stile and follow the fenced path as it leads between trees and carpets of bracken, dropping down to a footbridge. Ascend a steep bank to reach a stile and keep the fence on your right. Continue to a kissing gate and head towards Cuckfield's prominent church spire. On reaching South Street, turn left and return to the village centre.

WHERE TO EAT AND DRINK Cuckfield has the White Harte in South Street, serving hot and cold meals and bar snacks, as well as the Cuckfield Tea Rooms and Corner House for light refreshments.

WHAT TO SEE Cuckfield Park, established by an ironmaster in Elizabeth I's reign, was the home of the Sergison family. Later, it became a school and was open to the public. Now it is in private ownership. Keep an eye out for the striking gatehouse.

WHILE YOU'RE THERE You will identify several unexpected features in the centre of the village of Ansty. One is the Cuckfield Rural Parish Council map of rights of way in the area which shows the full route of the walk, and the village sign shows a stag watching a horse and its rider trying to climb a hilly path. Not surprisingly, the name Ansty means 'steep path to 'hilltop'.

On Ditchling's Downs

DISTANCE 5 miles (8km)   **MINIMUM TIME** 2hrs 30min

ASCENT/GRADIENT 600ft (183m) ▲▲▲   **LEVEL OF DIFFICULTY** +++

PATHS Field paths, bridleways and a stretch of road, several stiles

LANDSCAPE Downland slopes and pasture

SUGGESTED MAP AA Walker's Map 15 Brighton & The South Downs

START/FINISH Grid reference: TQ326152

DOG FRIENDLINESS Off lead on enclosed paths. On lead near Ditchling

PARKING Free car park at rear of village hall in Ditchling

PUBLIC TOILETS At car park

Ditchling is a picturesque village that attracts generations of tourists, and it's a popular stopping off point for walkers on the nearby South Downs Way. It shelters beneath the escarpment of the Downs, with rolling green hills and lush countryside enhancing its setting.

ATTRACTING ARTISTS

Over the years Ditchling's classic English village prettiness has attracted eminent figures from the world of theatre and entertainment. The 'Forces' Sweetheart', Dame Vera Lynn, settled in Ditchling; distinguished thespian Sir Donald Sinden spent his childhood here; and the actress Ellen Terry was a frequent visitor. *The Snowman* creator Raymond Briggs also lives locally.

During the early years of the 20th century Ditchling became a fashionable haunt of celebrated artists and craftsmen – among them the cartoonist Rowland Emett and the sculptor and typographer Eric Gill, both of whom moved to the village. Another member of this illustrious coterie was the calligrapher Edward Johnston, who was widely admired for his revival of the craft of formal lettering. Johnston moved to Ditchling in 1913 and lived there until his death in 1944. His most famous work is instantly recognisable to just about everyone in the country – the lettering and logo for the London Underground, distinguished by a circle with a line running through it.

Ditchling's written records date back to AD 765. Sometime after that, the manor passed into the royal hands of Alfred the Great and Edward the Confessor. The village's oldest building by far is the church, built mainly in the 13th century of local flint and imported Normandy stone. There are rare chalk carvings and a huge Norman treasure chest. During the Regency expansion of Brighton, the streets were busy with traffic en route to the resort. Horses were changed at The Bull inn prior to the steep pull up on to the Downs. Make a similar journey on foot and you enter a breezy world of wide skies and distant horizons.

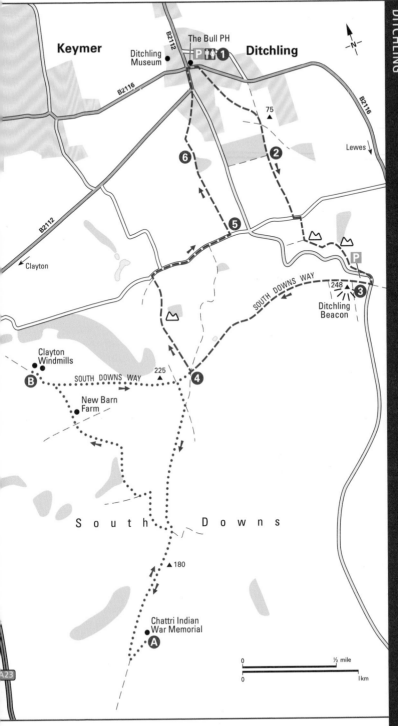

Keymer

Ditchling Museum

The Bull PH

P

1

Ditchling

B2112

B2116

B2116

Lewes

75

2

6

5

Clayton

Clayton Windmills

B

SOUTH DOWNS WAY

225

4

New Barn Farm

S o u t h

D o w n s

180

Chattri Indian War Memorial

A

P

248

3

Ditchling Beacon

SOUTH DOWNS WAY

0   ½ mile
0   1km

1 Turn right out of the car park and follow the B2116. Just after Charlton Gardens bear right, signposted to the Downs. The track divides by house no. 30: keep half left between hedges. Cross three pastures diagonally to the edge of woodland, walk along the wire fence to a stile and join a broad path through the woodland. Keep right at the fork by a bridleway waymark post. Pass a house and go straight ahead alongside a beech hedge where a concrete track runs off right.

2 Carry on along the track between trees, houses and gardens. On reaching the road, turn left and take the first track on the right. Ascend to a junction, fork left and climb the steep escarpment. Keep a breathtaking view of the Weald on your left. Further up, the path runs alongside the road. Look for the South Downs Way sign ahead and turn right across the road.

3 Skirt the right-hand side of the car park, through a gate and over Ditchling Beacon. Head west along the South Downs Way avoiding side turns, pass two dew ponds and reach a major junction of paths. Keymer is signposted to the right and Brighton to the left.

4 Follow the path north towards Keymer, with a fence on your left, and soon it descends quite steeply through a hummocky area of old chalkpits. Keep right at the signposted fork and make for a gate leading out to a lane. Bear left to the junction, then turn immediately right past a turning for Hassocks on the left. Walk along the lane, then take the waymarked footpath at the next stile on the left.

5 Follow the path along the left-hand edge of the field, go through two gates by some farm buildings and make for the gate ahead. Continue ahead along the right-hand field-edge and go through a gap in the field corner.

6 Cross the centre of the next field to a further gap and a waymarker post. Follow the defined path diagonally right to cross a footbridge and then a stile and follow the path out to the road. Immediately bear left by a grassy roundabout and take the path to the right of the sign for Neville Bungalows. Cut between trees, hedges and fences, following the narrow path to the road. Bear right towards Ditchling and walk back to the centre of the village, turning right into Lewes Road for the car park.

WHAT TO SEE Ditchling Beacon, although bleak and windswept in winter, is a delightful place. At 813ft (248m), it's the third highest point on the South Downs. The views are breathtaking and in good visibility you can see as far as the North Downs and the Ashdown Forest. Now in the care of the National Trust, the Beacon represented one of a chain of fires lit to warn of the Spanish Armada in 1588.

WHILE YOU'RE THERE Visit the Ditchling Museum, situated in the old school between the church and the pond. The history of Ditchling and its artists and craftsmen is illustrated in fascinating detail. Tools, country crafts and costumes are among the displays.

Chattri War Memorial and Clayton Windmills

DISTANCE 4.5 miles (7.2km)		MINIMUM TIME 1hr 45min (for this loop)		

ASCENT/GRADIENT 82ft (25m) ▲▲▲　　LEVEL OF DIFFICULTY ✚✚✚

PATHS Downland

SEE MAP AND INFORMATION PANEL FOR WALK 23

At Point ❹ keep ahead on the South Downs Way for a few paces and turn left at the sign 'Point 17 Stanmer & Ditchling Beacon'. Follow the path alongside the fence on your right to a gate, and continue across the field to the next gate where there is a path junction. Keep ahead on the same path for 0.5 miles (0.8km), through a gate where on the left you can see the Chattri Indian War Memorial, Point ❹, unusually sited on the downland slopes.

Very atmospheric, this memorial was erected to commemorate Sikh and Hindu soldiers of the Indian Army who fought during World War I. For those who did not survive the conflict, Brighton Corporation acquired this remote downland so that proper cremation rights could be given in accordance with their faith.

Retrace your steps 0.5 miles (0.8km) to the previous path junction and turn left. Follow the field boundary to a gate in the corner and turn right on an enclosed path. This turns left into a field; soon after turn right at the signpost, up the middle of the field. Climb quite steeply beside a golf course before joining the route of the South Downs Way on a track bend.

Continue ahead and pass alongside the outbuildings of New Barn Farm. Follow the South Downs Way until it turns sharp right and keep ahead towards the Clayton Windmills, Point ❸. Jack is a large brick-built tower mill which was worked until the early part of last century. Jill is a timber construction built at Brighton and conveyed to this site by teams of oxen in 1852. She has been carefully restored to working order and is open on Sunday and Bank Holiday afternoons in summer.

Head back up the track and keep left at the fork, where you rejoin the South Downs Way. Pass the path taken earlier to the right and turn left just beyond it signed 'Keymer'. Rejoin Walk 23 at Point ❹.

WHERE TO EAT AND DRINK The Bull at Ditchling, which dates from 1560, was once a courthouse and now serves food from an imaginative menu. Ditchling Museum's coffee shop serves snacks, and Ditchling Tea Room offers cream teas and evening meals.

Overleaf: Colourful merry-go-round at the funfair on Brighton's seafront (Walk 25)

A Stroll Around Brighton

DISTANCE 3 miles (4.8km)	MINIMUM TIME 2hrs 30min

ASCENT/GRADIENT 164ft (50m) ▲▲▲   LEVEL OF DIFFICULTY ✦✦✦

PATHS Pavements, streets, squares and promenade

LANDSCAPE The heart of Brighton and its famous seafront

SUGGESTED MAP AA Walker's Map 15 Brighton & The South Downs

START/FINISH Grid reference: TQ311049

DOG FRIENDLINESS On lead at all times

PARKING Various pay car parks close to station

PUBLIC TOILETS Several on seafront; Royal Pavilion Gardens

Brighton began life as a small fishing town, labouring under the name of 'Brighthelmstone', but it was Dr Richard Russell who really put it on the map in 1754 when he transformed the modest settlement into one of Britain's most famous resorts. Dr Russell believed fervently in the curative properties of seawater, and he began to promote Brighton as somewhere where the ailing could regain their health. Part of the cure included being towed out to the sea in horse-drawn bathing machines and plunged underwater by people employed as 'dippers'. It certainly caused a boom in the little fishing settlement, which became dubbed 'Doctor Brighton'. The Prince Regent, who later became George IV, helped to strengthen Brighton's new-found status by moving to a house which he then transformed into the Royal Pavilion. The town's genteel Regency terraces and graceful crescents reflect his influence on Brighton.

Later still, the railway era attracted visitors and holidaymakers in their thousands, boosting the town's economy to unprecedented new heights. As a seaside town Brighton has always been a mix of 'the raucous and the refined' – as one writer described it. It's cheeky but loveable; a place of fun and excitement. In 2000 the united boroughs of Brighton and Hove were awarded city status by the Queen, one of three millennium cities to be favoured in this way.

CHANGING MOODS

Brighton changes in mood from one quarter to the next. The main reminder of Brighton's fishing-town origins as 16th-century Brighthelmstone is in a knot of picturesque tiny streets and alleys known as The Lanes, just in from the sea front. Further north is the area known as the North Laine, with its strikingly individual shops and funky cafes. West of the Brighton Pier are Brunswick Square and Hove. To the east lies Kemp Town, with its grandiose seaside architecture reaching a climax at the elegant curves of Lewes Crescent.

THE ROYAL PAVILION

For sheer eccentricity, few buildings in Europe can rival the 18th-century Royal Pavilion. Even in the daytime, this Oriental fantasy, characterised by exuberant spires, minarets and onion domes, cannot escape your notice. Designed by the illustrious John Nash, it is Indian style outside, but inside the mood is of festive chinoiserie. Next door to it is the Dome, built in 1806, originally used as stables and a riding school for the Prince Regent. Across Pavilion Gardens, the Brighton Art Museum and Gallery is free to enter, and has an excellent section on the development of the town.

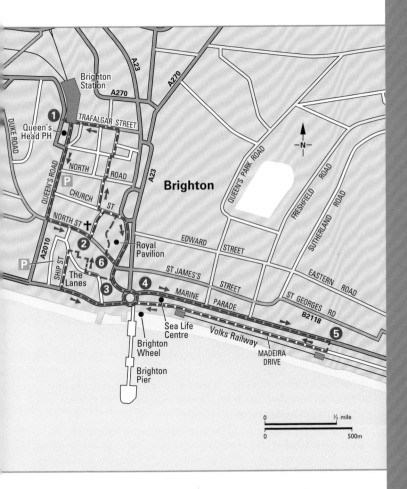

❶ From the front of Brighton Railway Station, keep the Queen's Head on the right and walk down Queen's Road, heading for the sea. Cross over North Road and continue down to the junction with North Street. Turn left here at the clock tower.

❷ Turn left into New Road. Pass the Theatre Royal on the left and on the right is the Brighton Dome Pavilion

Theatre. Note the striking facade of the Unitarian church. Bear right into Church Street and pass alongside the Corn Exchange, part of the Brighton Dome. Keep the Pavilion on your right, pass the George IV monument and veer right. Just after three art-deco bus shelters cross Castle Square into Old Steine and look for the YMCA and adjacent Marlborough House on the right. Originally built for the 4th Duke of Marlborough, the latter was sold in 1786 and later transformed by Robert Adam.

3 Turn right at some iron bollards, signposted 'The Lanes', and walk along a narrow lane. Cross over East Street and, just after the handsome town hall on the left (located in Bartholomews), bear right into Market Street, passing Nile Street. Continue into Brighton Place. You are in the district known as The Lanes. Veer left opposite the red-brick former 1835 House of Correction into Meeting House Lane, turning right at the junction in front of the Friends Meeting House entrance and keeping left at the next junction. Just after the Bath Arms, turn left into Union Street, then left again into Ship Street towards the seafront, where you can see the ruined West Pier on your right.

Veer left here and then continue to Brighton Pier.

4 Fork left by the Sea Life Centre and then follow Marine Parade. Pass Royal Crescent on the left, and the Madeira Lift on the right.

5 Opposite Bristol Court and Paston Place at a signpost to Kemptown, take the steps on the right, descending to the Volks Railway. Travel back to the terminus or return along the middle-level walkway to the Sea Life Centre. Cross into Old Steine and turn left into Castle Square.

6 Take the second right through the India Gateway and the Pavilion Gardens and past the Royal Pavilion and Museum and Art Gallery to another ornamental gateway. Turn left. Pass the Royal Pavilion and turn left into Church Street. Turn right into Gardner Street, through the funky North Laine area, and follow signs to the station, turning right and immediately left at the end into Kensington Gardens. Turn right and then left into Sydney Street, and left up Trafalgar Street to return to the station.

WHERE TO EAT AND DRINK With over 400 restaurants in Brighton and Hove, and countless pubs and bars, there are numerous possibilities for eating and drinking along this walk.

WHAT TO SEE The clock tower, at the junction of Queen's Road and North Street, was erected in 1888 to commemorate Queen Victoria's Jubilee the year before. The clock face has gilt Roman numerals and a gilt time-ball designed to rise and fall precisely on the hour. West Pier is one of Brighton's most famous landmarks, though it has been in a poor state of repair for some years.

WHILE YOU'RE THERE Dating back to 1869, the Sea Life Centre is the largest in Britain, with many displays of live creatures. Alternatively, you can take a ride on the Volks Railway. Built by electrical pioneer Marcus Volk and opened in 1883, it was the first public electric railway in Britain.

The Deans – Rottingdean, Ovingdean and Roedean

DISTANCE 5 miles (8km)   MINIMUM TIME 2hrs

ASCENT/GRADIENT 305ft (93m) ▲▲▲   LEVEL OF DIFFICULTY ✦✦✦

PATHS Busy village streets, downland paths and tracks

LANDSCAPE Rolling downland extending to the sea

SUGGESTED MAP AA Walker's Map 15 Brighton & The South Downs

START/FINISH Grid reference: TQ347032

DOG FRIENDLINESS On lead in Rottingdean. Under careful control in places

PARKING Free car park at Roedean Bottom, at junction of A259 and B2006

PUBLIC TOILETS Rottingdean village and the Undercliff

Although just along the coast from Brighton, Rottingdean preserves its village character, with its old houses, pond and church huddled beneath the windmill on the downs. Not surprisingly it has long been considered a very desirable place in which to live.

HOLLOW RING

Rottingdean is one of seven Saxon settlements on this stretch of the Sussex coast, all ending in 'dean'. The word 'dean' or 'dene' means hollow or valley of the South Downs. The Deans is the collective name for them and, apart from Roedean, the famous public school for girls, Rottingdean is probably the most well known. Despite expanding development over the years, the village still retains the feel of an independent community. But there's a lot more to Rottingdean than historic buildings and landmarks.

Start the walk by following the scenic Undercliff, with its close-up view of the sea, then look for a comprehensive information board at the junction of the High Street and the A259 which helps you to identify what's what and who lived where as you explore the village streets. The Black Horse was said to have been a meeting place for smugglers, while Whipping Post House was the home of Captain Dunk, the local butcher and a renowned bootlegger.

Rudyard Kipling lived at The Elms in Rottingdean until driven away by inquisitive fans and autograph hunters. He wrote *Kim* and the *Just So* stories here, among other works. Kipling loved the South Downs and he found these hills a great source of inspiration. 'Our blunt, bow-headed, whalebacked Downs', he wrote in his famous poem *Sussex*. Part of his garden is now Kipling Gardens, a beautiful park in the village centre, open to all.

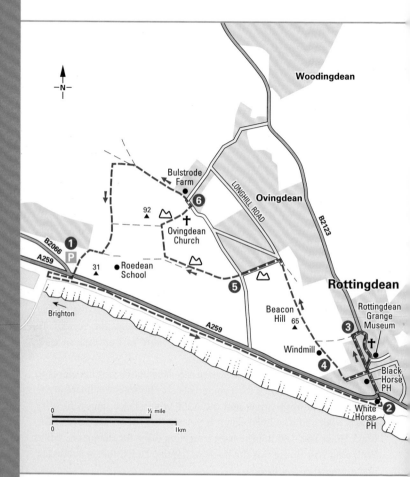

Some of Kipling's relatives had local associations and it was here in the village that his cousin Stanley Baldwin met and married Lucy Ridsdale, whose family lived at The Dene. Baldwin was a Conservative statesman who, as Prime Minister, secured three terms in office during the 1920s and 30s. The flint church at Rottingdean is noted for its impressive stained-glass windows designed by the Pre-Raphaelite artist Sir Edward Burne-Jones, who lived at North End House on the west side of the green. Enid Bagnold, who wrote the famous novel *National Velvet*, was also a local resident.

❶ From the car park cross the A259 and turn right towards Brighton, following the path parallel to the road. Look for the path on the left and follow it down to the Undercliff. Head east towards Rottingdean, passing a toilet block and a cafe, and continue

on the path until you reach buildings, including Highcliff Court.

❷ Turn left into the village and pass the White Horse pub on the left. Cross the A259 into Rottingdean High Street. Pass the Black Horse, Nevill

Road and Steyning Road and continue along the street. As you approach The Green, look for The Dene and then Kipling Gardens on the right.

3 Follow the road round to the right and to a T-junction, then keep right and head back into Rottingdean village. Pass the war memorial and the village pond and look for the church on the left. Pass the Plough Inn and walk back down to the High Street. Turn left, then right into Nevill Road, climb quite steeply and bear right into Sheep Walk. Look to the right here for a good view of the village and its church.

4 Keep the windmill on your left and follow the bridleway along the downland ridge. Woodingdean can be glimpsed in the distance, and the buildings of Ovingdean are seen in the foreground. The outline of Roedean School is visible against the horizon. Continue to Beacon Hill, turn left and walk down to the junction.

5 Cross over to a gate, then go along the fence to a second gate. Follow the fence on the right which bends right. Soon after, cross to the other side at a gate and continue in the same direction uphill along the fence. Pass a private path to Roedean School and continue beside the wire fence to a stile in the field corner. Turn right and skirt the pasture to turn right over the next stile. Descend steeply towards Ovingdean church, cutting off the field corner to reach a stile. Cross into the field and keep the churchyard wall hard by you on the right.

6 Cross a stile to the lychgate and walk down to the junction. Turn left and, when the road bends right at Bulstrode Farm, go straight on along a wide concrete track, following the bridleway. Keep left at the fork, then immediately left again at the next fork a few paces beyond. Just after the track swings sharply to the left and is about to go up through a gate, keep forward alongside the fence on the left. The car park by the A259 looms into view now. When you reach the road, by the entrance to Roedean School, cross the grass to the car park.

WHERE TO EAT AND DRINK Along the Undercliff, you'll find a cafe open at weekends throughout the year. In Rottingdean are several tea rooms, a fish and chip shop and a cluster of pubs, including the Black Horse and the Plough.

WHAT TO SEE As you descend to the Undercliff, look for the buildings of Brighton Marina. This is one of Europe's largest purpose-built yacht harbours, with moorings for several thousand boats. Founded in 1855, Roedean School moved to its present site in the late 1890s from Sussex Square in Brighton. During World War II the school relocated to Keswick in the Lake District to avoid any threat of enemy attack. At various stages along the walk there are small stones to be seen beside the path, bearing the initials RS and the date – 1938. There is no record of these stones in the school archives, though they might be some form of boundary marker.

WHILE YOU'RE THERE Visit Rottingdean Grange Museum. Originally the vicarage, the Grange used to be the home of the artist Sir William Nicholson, who lived here prior to World War I. The building was enlarged by Sir Edwin Lutyens and now includes a gallery, museum and Tea Garden. Among the exhibits is a reconstruction of Rudyard Kipling's study.

Overleaf: View from the Fulking Escarpment on the South Downs Way (Walk 27)

Grand Views from Devil's Dyke

DISTANCE 2.75 miles (4.4km)	MINIMUM TIME 1hr 30min
ASCENT/GRADIENT 656ft (200m) ▲▲▲	LEVEL OF DIFFICULTY ✦✦✦

PATHS Field and woodland paths

LANDSCAPE Chalk grassland, steep escarpment and woodland

SUGGESTED MAP AA Walker's Map 15 Brighton & The South Downs

START/FINISH Grid reference: TQ269111

DOG FRIENDLINESS Mostly off lead. On lead on approach to Poynings

PARKING Devil's Dyke Summer Down free car park

PUBLIC TOILETS By Devil's Dyke pub

Sussex is rich in legend and folklore and the Devil and his fiendish works crop up all over the county. The local landmark of Devil's Dyke is a prime example – perfectly blending the natural beauty of the South Downs with the mystery and originality of ancient mythology. Few other fables in this part of the country seem to have caught the public imagination in quite the same way.

DISTURBED BY A CANDLE

Devil's Dyke is a geological quirk, a spectacular, steep-sided downland combe or cleft 300ft (91m) deep and half a mile (800m) long. According to legend, it was dug by the Devil as part of a trench extending to the sea. The idea was to try to flood the area with sea water and, in so doing, destroy the churches of the Weald. However, the story goes that the Devil was disturbed by a woman carrying a candle. Mistaking this for the dawn, he quickly disappeared, leaving his work unfinished. The reality of how Devil's Dyke came to be is probably less interesting. No one knows for sure how it originated, but it is most likely to have been cut by glacial meltwaters when the ground was permanently frozen in the Ice Age. Rising to over 600ft (180m), this famous beauty spot is also a magnificent viewpoint where the views stretch for miles in all directions. The Clayton Windmills are visible on a clear day, as are Chanctonbury Ring, Haywards Heath and parts of the Ashdown Forest. The artist Constable described this view as the grandest in the world.

Devil's Dyke has long been a tourist honeypot. During the Victorian era and in the early part of the 20th century, the place was akin to a bustling theme park with a cable car crossing the valley and a steam railway coming up from Brighton. On Whit Monday 1893 a staggering 30,000 people visited Devil's Dyke. In 1928 HRH the Duke of York dedicated the Dyke Estate for the use of the public forever and in fine

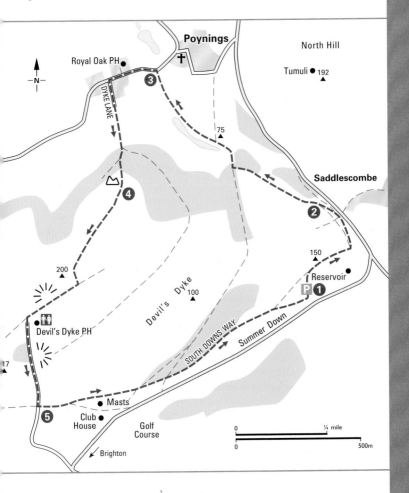

weather it can seem just as crowded as it was in Queen Victoria's day, assuming the feel of a seaside resort at the height of the season. Hang-gliders swoop silently over the grassy downland like pterodactyls and kite flyers spill from their cars in search of fun and excitement. But the views more than make up for the invasion of visitors, and away from the chalk slopes and the car park the walk soon heads for more peaceful surroundings.

Beginning on Summer Down, on the route of the South Downs Way, you drop down gradually to the village of Poynings where there may be time for a welcome pint at the Royal Oak. Rest and relax for as long as you can here because it's a long, steep climb to the Devil's Dyke pub. The last leg of the walk is gentle and relaxing by comparison.

❶ With the road behind you, take the kissing gate on the right side of the car park, go down across the grass for a few paces., then turn right on a path

(the South Downs Way) which you follow, soon passing a railing round a covered grass-topped reservoir. Soon the path curves left and drops down to the road. Part company with the South Downs Way at this point, as it crosses over to join the private road to Saddlescombe Farm, and follow the verge for about 75yds (68m). Bear left at the footpath sign and drop down the bank to a stile.

2 Follow the line of the tarmac lane as it curves right to reach a waymark. Leave the lane and walk ahead alongside power lines, keeping the line of trees and bushes on the right. Eventually veer right into the vegetation and cross a stile. Drop down into the woods and turn right at a junction with a bridleway. Past a pond, reach a path junction at the edge of the wood and fork left between fields and a wooded dell; pass over a stile and soon bear left over a footbridge to a signposted stile. Turn right towards Poynings.

3 Head for a gate and footpath sign and cross the road, turning left along the parallel path along to the Royal Oak and then in to Dyke Lane on the left. There is a memorial stone here, dedicated to the memory of George Stephen Cave Cuttress, a resident of Poynings for over 50 years. Follow the tarmac bridleway and soon it narrows to a path. On reaching the fork, by a National Trust sign for Devil's Dyke, veer right and begin climbing the steps.

4 Follow the path up to a gate and at the fork continue up the stairs. From the higher ground there are breathtaking views to the north and west. Carry on to a kissing gate and head up the slope towards the Devil's Dyke pub, keeping it to your left. Take the road round to the left past the pub car park, walking along the footway beside the left side of the road past a bridleway sign, and look to the left for a definitive view of Devil's Dyke.

5 At a National Trust sign for Summer Down turn left on the South Downs Way. Follow the trail, keeping Devil's Dyke down to your left, and eventually reach Summer Down car park.

WHERE TO EAT AND DRINK The Royal Oak, located in the centre of Poynings, includes a patio and gardens for warm days and offers home-cooked specialities, local seafood, cask ales and summer barbeques. The Devil's Dyke pub, three-quarters of the way round the walk, has a family dining area and garden patio. Sunday lunch, baguettes and salads feature on the menu.

WHAT TO SEE Devil's Dyke consists of 183 acres (74ha) of open downland which is home to all manner of flora and fauna, including horseshoe vetch, the Pride of Sussex flower and the common spotted orchid. The adonis blue butterfly also inhabits the area. The Dyke lies within the South Downs Area of Outstanding Natural Beauty and is a designated Site of Special Scientific Interest. (SSSI).

WHILE YOU'RE THERE Take a stroll through the village of Poynings, pronounced 'Punnings' locally. The village takes its name from the Poynages family, who held the manor here during the Middle Ages. Michael de Poynages, a one-time lord of the manor, left 200 marcs (£2,400) in his will towards the building of the 14th-century Church of Holy Trinity.

Bramber and Beeding Bridge

DISTANCE 2.5 miles (4km)	MINIMUM TIME 1hr 15min
ASCENT/GRADIENT Negligible ▲▲▲	LEVEL OF DIFFICULTY ✛✛✛

PATHS Riverside, field and village paths, some road walking

LANDSCAPE Adur Valley flood plain

SUGGESTED MAP AA Leisure Map 23 Brighton & The South Downs

START/FINISH Grid reference: TQ185105

DOG FRIENDLINESS Take care on approach to Beeding Bridge and in Bramber

PARKING Free car park at Bramber Castle

PUBLIC TOILETS At car park in The Street, Bramber

Crossing Beeding Bridge, which is recorded in documents as dating back to the reign of Henry III, it is worth stopping for a few moments to consider its importance as a river crossing. Not only does the bridge play a vital part in this walk, allowing you to cross the River Adur easily from one bank to the other, but more than 350 years ago, in October 1651, it enabled Charles II, defeated and on the run, to escape his enemies and eventually flee to safety in France.

PURSUED BY PARLIAMENT

His route through the Adur Valley was one step on a long and eventful journey that has became an integral part of British history. Following the Battle of Worcester, where his army was soundly beaten, the young Charles fled across England, hotly pursued by Parliamentary forces under the leadership of Oliver Cromwell. Though documented fact, it has all the hallmarks of a classic adventure story, a colourful, rip-roaring tale of intrigue and suspense.

First, he made his way north, intending to cross the River Severn into Wales where he could find a ship and sail to the continent. But the river was heavily guarded and Charles was forced to change his plans.

Instead he travelled south through the Cotswolds and the Mendips, eventually reaching Charmouth on the Dorset coast. Once again his plans to escape by boat fell through and, in a desperate attempt to avoid capture, he made his way along the South Coast to Shoreham near Brighton, where at last he found a ship which could take him to France. His journey through England lasted six weeks and during that crucial period he was loyally supported by his followers, many at great risk to their own lives.

The King's arrival in Bramber was one heart-stopping moment among many during his time on the run. As he and his escort came into the village from the west, they were horrified to find many troopers in the vicinity of the riverbank. Charles realised they had been posted here to guard Beeding Bridge, which was his only means of reaching Shoreham easily. Cautiously, he crossed the bridge and continued on his way undetected. Moments later, the Royal party looked round to see a group of cavalry hotly pursuing them across country. Charles feared the worst, but as they reached him, the soldiers suddenly overtook the King and rode off into the distance. Fortunately for Charles, they had been pursuing someone else on that occasion. After their narrow escape in the Adur valley, the group decided it was safer to split up and make their own way to the coast.

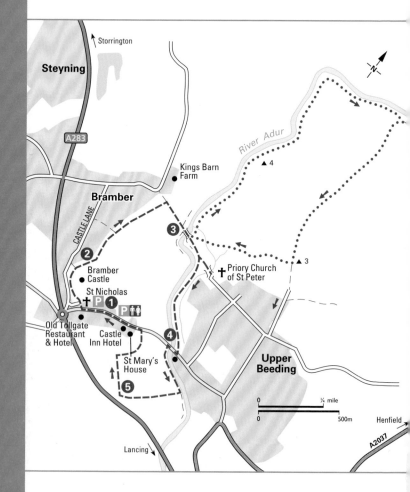

❶ Facing the castle and wooded ramparts, locate the narrow path in the left-hand corner of the parking area and follow it left as it meanders through the trees to the left of the castle ramparts. Keep right up the slope at a fork, then bear left downhill at the next fork to reach a track.

② Turn right and head up through the trees, passing galvanised gates on the left and right. The rooftops of houses and bungalows peep into view along here. Continue ahead at the next signpost and the River Adur can be glimpsed between the trees on the right. Pass a footpath on the left and make for a stile ahead. Follow the path on the right of the field to the next stile and turn right towards the footbridge spanning the Adur.

③ Cross the bridge and bear right, following the riverbank towards Upper Beeding. Branch off left to a footbridge and and steps leading up to the Priory Church of St Peter. Returning to the main walk, continue along the riverbank path towards Upper Beeding and Beeding Bridge.

④ Cross the road and turn right over the footbridge, then left along the right-hand bank, heading downstream. Continue to a kissing gate and turn right. Keep the fence on the right and, at the fence corner, go straight on out across the field.

⑤ As you approach the A283, turn right in front of the kissing gate and head towards the trees, with the ruins of Bramber Castle peeping through. Make for a kissing gate and bear right. Follow the track which bends left and, just before it bends right, turn left through a gate and right along a tarmac drive running through the trees to the road. Turn left, pass St Mary's House and walk along the High Street, passing the Castle Inn Hotel and village car park. On reaching the Old Tollgate Restaurant and Hotel, cross the road and follow the steps up to the church and car park.

WHAT TO SEE Overlooking the Adur Valley and just off the walk is Sele Priory, established by William de Braose. Sele is another name for Beeding. The vicarage now occupies the site of the old priory, part of an ancient Benedictine foundation, and next to it is the Priory Church of St Peter.

WHILE YOU'RE THERE Before starting the walk, have a look at the ruins of Bramber Castle. Now in the care of English Heritage and the National Trust, it was built just after the Norman Conquest to defend the exposed and vulnerable Sussex coast. The castle was held by the de Braose family until 1326 when it passed to Alice de Bohun and then to her eldest son. Later, during the Civil War, it was badly assaulted by the Roundheads. Nowadays, all that remains of it is the 70ft (21m) high gateway. At the centre of the site is evidence of a motte which might have borne a timber tower. Next to Bramber Castle is the Parish Church of St Nicholas, originally the castle chapel. Like the castle, this building also suffered in battle. Cromwell's men apparently used it as a gun emplacement, causing extensive damage to the nave and tower. Towards the end of the walk, you pass the entrance to St Mary's House in Bramber. This splendid medieval building is one of the village's proudest features and the best example of late 15th-century timber framing in Sussex. One of the highlights of a tour of the house is seeing the unique printed room, decorated for the visit of Queen Elizabeth I.

Upper Beeding and Along the River Adur

DISTANCE 2.5 miles (4km)   MINIMUM TIME 1hr 15min

ASCENT/GRADIENT Negligible ▲▲▲   LEVEL OF DIFFICULTY ✚✚✚

SEE MAP AND INFORMATION PANEL FOR WALK 28

To extend Walk 28 and follow the River Adur a little further upstream, cross over the stile and bridge at Point ❸ and go left. Cross five more stiles; beyond them electricity pylons can be seen marching across the landscape, with the lovely Adur sweeping to the right. Follow the riverbank and make for the next galvanised gate and accompanying stile. Approach some light woodland and turn right just before it, at a fingerpost.

Head south now, with the buildings of Bramber and Upper Beeding ahead. The distinctive outline of Lancing College's vast, cathedral-like chapel and its vaulted roof of stone and chalk can be seen against the skyline. The chapel was begun in 1867, and work was eventually completed in 1978, after more than a century.

Veer slightly right as you steer a path across this open, low-lying ground. Make for two stiles and cross a bridge. Maintain the same direction and cross two stiles in quick succession. Walk along a reed-fringed waterway to the next stile and continue ahead, following the footpath fingerpost. Join a track, taking the next footpath

on the right. Go round a gate, cross over a paddock to a second gate, then cross the plank bridges and a stile to pass into the next field.

(After heavy rain it can be flooded at this point. If there is too much water, return to the track and turn right. The track becomes a road and leads past houses to a crossroads with a footpath sign on the left. Turn right along Pepperscombe Lane and at the end continue in the same direction along Church Lane to the Priory Church of St Peter. Pass the church and keep ahead, descending steps to cross a footbridge. Carry on to join the riverbank path a short distance southeast of Point ❸. Turn left and continue on the main route.)

If the route is accessible, follow the clear path back towards the Adur, with this stretch of the walk providing an unexpected view of the tower of the priory, seen peeping through the trees. Continue across the meadows, which offer a clearer impression of the site, and soon you reach the footbridge. Stay on this side of the river, turn left and follow the directions from Point ❸ to Beeding Bridge.

WHERE TO EAT AND DRINK The Castle Inn Hotel in Bramber has a good menu with a choice of platters and mains, as well as sandwiches. The Old Tollgate Hotel's award winning Carvery Restaurant serves a choice of locally sourced seasonal food.

Parham's Stately Park

DISTANCE 5.5 miles (8.8km)	MINIMUM TIME 2hrs 30min

ASCENT/GRADIENT 640ft (195m) ▲▲▲   LEVEL OF DIFFICULTY +++

PATHS Bridleways, parkland paths, and drives and stretches of road

LANDSCAPE Elegant parkland and steep escarpment

SUGGESTED MAP AA Walker's Map 20 Chichester & The South Downs

START/FINISH Grid reference: TQ051144

DOG FRIENDLINESS On lead in Parham Park, in vicinity of B2139 and below Kithurst Hill car park

PARKING Rackham Old School free car park

PUBLIC TOILETS Parham House (visitors to the house and gardens only)

The magnificent Elizabethan mansion of Parham House is one of the great treasures of Sussex, recalling the days of weekend house parties, servants below stairs and gracious living – a way of life that has all but disappeared. The wonderful setting, deer park and views of the South Downs enhance Parham's beauty and little has changed here since Tudor times. It was in 1540, at the Dissolution of the Abbey of Westminster, that Henry VIII granted the manor of Parham to Robert Palmer, a London mercer. Years later, in 1577, his great grandson, aged just two and a half, laid the foundation stone of the present larger house, which was built to incorporate the old one. The little boy's mother was a god-daughter of Elizabeth I and it is believed the Queen dined here in 1593. The 875-acre (354ha) estate was sold in 1601, and then again in 1922 when it was purchased by the younger son of Viscount Cowdray. The new owners opened Parham to the public for the first time in 1948 – an unusual step in the lean, post-war years. The house has been open to the public ever since and is now owned by a charitable trust.

GARDENS AND PARKLAND

Parham's gardens consist of 7 acres (3ha) of landscaped Pleasure Grounds and a colourful 4-acre (1.6ha) Walled Garden. When the house is open, large quantities of flowers are cut from the garden each week for the fresh flower arrangements which brighten the rooms. The Herb Garden grows medieval and Tudor medicinal and culinary herbs, while the orchard contains traditional varieties of apple and other fruit trees. Parham means 'pear tree settlement', but the fruit most associated with Parham is the Golden Pippin Apple, which is thought to have originated here in 1629.

Of particular note in the Park are the many ancient, mature and veteran trees. A veteran tree contains significant quantities of dead wood or decaying limbs. Several oak trees are over 500 years old and rare lichens flourish on the bark. A distinctive feature of the Park is the abundant mistletoe growing high up in the lime trees.

You'll see the house and Park from the top of the South Downs on this enjoyable circuit. Look out for the 18th-century dovecote when you walk through the Park. This has over 650 brick-built nesting boxes inside. Over the centuries, the pigeons would have provided the Parham household with a regular source of fresh meat, particularly during the winter. Pigeon pie was a popular delicacy.

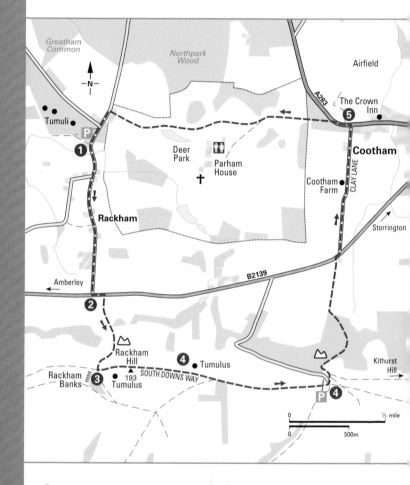

1 On leaving the car park turn right and head towards the dramatic scarp of the South Downs. Pass Rackham Road and follow the lane into the village of Rackham. Keep on the road as it cuts between fields to reach a junction.

2 Bear left here and, taking care, follow the busy and fast B2139 for about 75yds (68m). Turn right to join a bridleway and climb steeply, passing through a gate. Continue the steep ascent. Glancing back at intervals will reveal views of Parham Park in the distance and, away to the west, the meandering River Arun. The path curves to the right and from this high ground much of the route of the walk can be seen. Amberley, with its imposing castle remains, is also visible from this lofty vantage point. Keep ahead to a bridle gate, ignoring a stile and gate over to your right, and join the South Downs Way.

3 Turn left along the South Downs Way ridge-top track and head east. Pass a trig point on the right and continue ahead across Rackham Hill. Parham House can be seen down to your left, while over to the right on a clear day you can spot the sea glinting in the sunshine. Pass through a belt of trees and continue to Kithurst Hill car park on the left. Branch off here by double galvanised gates.

4 With the car park sign on the left, go forward to join a bridleway which initially runs parallel to the road. Follow the path to a gate, cross a pasture to a second gate and follow the path as it descends quite steeply between trees and undergrowth. Ignoring a gated track on your right, keep ahead past rows of conifers. Join a track bearing left and soon turn

right passing alongside a line of trees, with a field on the right. Follow the track to reach a wooden gate leading out to the road by a house called Paygate. Turn right and then left along Clay Lane, passing Cootham Farm and Lower Barn to reach a junction with the A283. To visit Cootham and The Crown Inn, turn right.

5 Walk back along the main road past Clay Lane. Make for the entrance to Parham Park, pass a stone-built lodge and go through a gate leading into the deer park. Follow the drive and, when it curves gently to the left, join a waymarked parallel path on the right. Cross a pasture and look away to the south to take in a striking view of Parham House with the scarp of the Downs rising steeply behind it. On reaching a junction of drives head straight on, soon passing alongside a stone wall on your left with a lake beyond it. Continue through the gently undulating parkland and turn left when you get to the road by West Lodges. Pass a stone house and ignore a turning to Greatham and Coldwaltham on the right. Follow the lane down through the trees, back to the car park.

WHERE TO EAT AND DRINK The Crown Inn at Cootham offers a good selection of snacks and main meals. Rack of lamb and game casserole feature on the menu, and there are cask ales and a beer garden. Parham Park includes refreshments such as light lunches and cream teas. There is also a picnic area.

WHAT TO SEE The fallow deer here are descendants of the original herd first mentioned in 1628. The little church in the park, dedicated to St Peter, was built in 1545 and almost totally rebuilt between 1800 and 1820. Up until this time, Parham was very isolated and inaccessible, with no proper roads to enable visitors to reach the estate. The small village around the church virtually disappeared at the end of the 18th century, helping to maintain the privacy of Parham House.

WHILE YOU'RE THERE Tour the richly decorated Tudor Parham House, built during the reign of Henry VIII. The exhibition in the Ship Room shows the roles Parham played from 1922 onwards, and the restoration of the house: from fashionable country club to its role in World War II, and later as a home for 'mentally frail old ladies'.

Hilaire Belloc's Shipley

DISTANCE 7 miles (11.3km)	MINIMUM TIME 3hrs

ASCENT/GRADIENT 98ft (30m) ▲▲▲   LEVEL OF DIFFICULTY ✦✦✦

PATHS Field and woodland paths, country roads, several stiles

LANDSCAPE Undulating farmland and parkland

SUGGESTED MAP AA Leisure Map 23 Brighton & The South Downs

START/FINISH Grid reference: TQ143219

DOG FRIENDLINESS Off lead on drives and farm tracks. Under control through Knepp Castle Estate Deer Park and near A24

PARKING Small free car park at Shipley

PUBLIC TOILETS None on route

It has been said that Hilaire Belloc is to Sussex what Wordsworth is to the Lake District. He was certainly passionate about the county and this delightful walk suggests more than a hint of the great man's spirit.

MAN OF LETTERS

Belloc was a distinguished man of letters – a poet, writer, historian and politician in his time – and exploring the picturesque countryside surrounding his Shipley home, savouring the beauty of the landscape, you really feel that you are following in his illustrious footsteps. Born in France in 1870, to an English mother and a French father, Belloc spent much of his childhood at Slindon near Arundel, before serving in the French artillery. He then attended Oxford University where he was an outstanding Union debater. He forged friendships with some of the leading figures of the day and made, too, some notable enemies including Herbert Asquith, Lloyd George and HG Wells.

Belloc is best remembered as a writer of more than a hundred works. Many were inspired by his extensive travels – some of them describing extraordinary feats of endurance. He crossed the United States of America on foot to propose to a Californian girl that he had fallen in love with when he was 19 years old. In later life he walked through France, over the Alps and down to Rome in an effort to meet the Pope. He failed due to an administrative mix-up but recorded the journey in a book, *The Path to Rome*. In 1902 he made another marathon journey walking from Robertsbridge in the east of Sussex to Harting in the west – a distance of some 90 miles (145.8km), and wrote the classic tale, *The Four Men* – a reference to himself and three fictional characters who accompany him on the journey. It is written with the passion of a man who fears that what he most loves in the world may soon fade and die.

Belloc bought King's Land in Shipley in 1906 and remained there until his death in 1953. The house was a shop when he bought it for the princely sum of £900. The walk crosses peaceful parkland to reach the village of West Grinstead (not to be confused with the much larger East Grinstead) and then crosses the River Adur to Dial Post. From here it's a pleasant country walk back to Shipley, passing Belloc's charming old windmill.

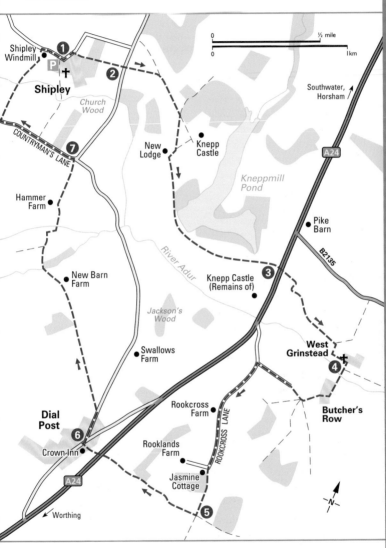

1 From the car park turn right and follow the road round the left bend. After 100yds (91m) bear right through a kissing gate and follow the right-hand boundary of the field. Look for a gate into Church Wood. Follow the path through the trees through the trees, ignoring the permissive footpath turns. Go through a gate and continue along the edge of the field to the road.

2 Cross over and follow a path through trees to a gate and enter parkland. Walk ahead to reach a footpath fingerpost. Bear right and follow the drive towards Knepp Castle. On reaching a left turning, swing right and head across the pasture. On reaching a drive, turn right and pass New Lodge. Follow the drive as it runs alongside Kneppmill Pond. The remains of the original Knepp Castle, designed by John Nash in 1809, can be seen across the fields.

3 Cross the A24 and locate a footpath sign and gate just past the bus stop. Walk ahead to a footbridge in the right-hand corner of the field. The woodland path bears right and soon left by a stile and continues along the right-hand side of the field. At the hedge corner keep ahead for about 75yds (68m) to a footpath sign and bear right. Follow the hedge to a gate leading into the churchyard, pass the church door and turn right at the footpath sign.

4 Make for a kissing gate situated in the corner of the churchyard and follow the paved path south. Cross the River Adur, bearing left to a gate and a concrete track which becomes a tarmac drive as it passes through the hamlet of Butcher's Row. Follow it in a southwesterly direction, keeping right when you reach a junction with two tracks and a footpath. Bear left at the next junction and follow Rookcross Lane. Pass Rookcross Farm on your right, go through a gate and keep to the metalled drive for 0.5 miles (800m), passing Jasmine Cottage, before veering right at a private drive sign to Hobshorts.

5 Follow the left-hand edge of the field to a fingerpost in the first corner. Enter the next field and turn right, keeping to the field-edge. Keep to the boundary, pass some oak trees and drop down beside woodland to cross a plank bridge. Keep to the left boundary of the next field to the stile in the corner and recross the busy A24. Cross a stile and follow the footpath over pasture to a junction. Turn left through the gate into a field, pass a bungalow and turn right. The path leads to the Crown Inn garden and car park.

6 Turn right on leaving the pub, walk through Dial Post and veer left into Swallows Lane. Once clear of the village, branch off to the left and follow the straight farm road to New Barn Farm, where the track kinks left and right. Ignore a footpath turn to the left and another further on and continue along the track to the road.

7 Turn left into Countryman's Lane and pass a footpath that leads to the church. Continue to the next right-hand bridleway. Follow the path to Shipley Windmill, then continue to the road and turn right for the car park.

WHERE TO EAT AND DRINK The Crown Inn at Dial Post serves good food made with locally sourced produce wherever possible.

WHILE YOU'RE THERE Although Shipley Windmill is no longer open to visitors, it may be viewed externally from the adjacent public bridleway. The largest windmill in Sussex, it was built in 1879 and acquired by Hilaire Belloc in 1906. He called the mill 'Mrs Shipley' and used to raise his hat to it. Following Belloc's death, an appeal was launched to restore it and by 1991 Shipley Mill was in full working order. The BBC filmed parts of the television series *Jonathan Creek*, starring Alan Davies, at the mill.

Loxwood's Forgotten Canal

DISTANCE 4.5 miles (7.2km)	MINIMUM TIME 2hrs

ASCENT/GRADIENT 82ft (25m) ▲▲▲   LEVEL OF DIFFICULTY ✦✦✦

PATHS Field paths, tracks and tow path, several stiles

LANDSCAPE Gentle farmland bisected by Wey and Arun Junction Canal

SUGGESTED MAP AA Walker's Map 23 Guildford, Farnham & The Downs

START/FINISH Grid reference: TQ042311

DOG FRIENDLINESS On lead on road and stretches of farmland

PARKING Free car park by Wey and Arun Junction Canal, next to Onslow Arms, Loxwood, beyond pub car park and Canal Centre

PUBLIC TOILETS Disabled toilet at Canal Centre

The Wey and Arun Junction Canal was completed in 1816 to connect the Wey and Arun rivers and form part of a continuous inland waterway route, linking London with the south coast. Glancing at derelict stretches of the 23-mile (37km) canal today, in places either completely dried up or engulfed by weeds and a sea of mud, you could be forgiven for thinking that 'derelict' is perhaps an understatement.

CANAL MAKEOVER

Journey along the canal tow path a little further, however, and you'll see that a makeover is taking place. After years of neglect, a great deal of restoration work has already been completed along the route of the old canal and a stretch beyond the Onslow Arms has now been fully restored, with boat trips offered at weekends, and two new locks have been constructed to take the canal underneath the modern B2133. But there is a great deal still to do if the Wey and Arun Canal Trust is to realise its dream of reopening this stretch of what became known as 'London's lost route to the sea'.

During the 19th century it was possible to travel by boat from London to Littlehampton on the Sussex coast via Weybridge, Guildford, Pulborough and Arundel. This route represented a tiny but important part of a once complex and extensive network of inland waterways covering England and Wales. To make that journey involved travelling along the rivers Wey and Arun which were linked between Shalford in Surrey and Pallingham in Sussex by the Wey and Arun Junction Canal and the Arun Navigation.

Though the canal was initially successful, the arrival of the railways spelled its demise. It finally closed in 1871, and as the years passed the waterway clogged up and was reduced to a stagnant depression in the ground, remaining in that state for the best part of a century, abandoned and largely forgotten. The lock by Devil's Hole, an abandoned oxbow of canal that was an earlier attempt to bypass a slope, was used by Canadians in World War II for target practice.

A LABOUR OF LOVE

In the early 1970s a group of dedicated volunteers and canal enthusiasts formed the Wey and Arun Canal Trust, with the aim of restoring the canal as a public amenity, including its diverse range of wildlife habitats. Many of the original bridges and locks have been restored, but construction work of this kind is very expensive. The conservation project depends on the Trust's fundraising efforts and the goodwill of local councils, businesses and landowners. This pretty walk begins in Loxwood and gives an insight into the rebirth of the Wey and Arun Junction Canal. Heading north, the route eventually joins the tow path, and you'll see how the conservation programme is transforming the canal from an overgrown ditch into a vibrant waterway.

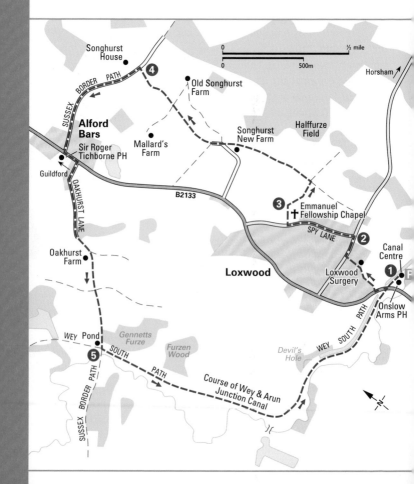

1 Walk past the Canal Centre and the Onslow Arms to the B2133. Turn right, cross over the canal, continue on the road for 50yds (41m), and then turn right along a signposted path leading between hedges. At a road, keep ahead, Loxwood Surgery to the right. Turn right at the T-junction.

2 Pass Burley Close and turn left into Spy Lane. Follow the road as it leads between houses and look for the Emmanuel Fellowship Chapel on the right. Bear right immediately beyond the chapel, over a stile, and skirt the Emmanuel Fellowship playing field.

3 Follow the path to the next stile and pass through a tongue of woodland. Make for the right-hand boundary of the field, then keep ahead to a stile in the corner. Turn right and immediately left by a fingerpost and stile. Follow the left-hand edge of three fields, passing Songhurst New Farm. Head for the field corner and look for a stile just to the right of a galvanised gate. Continue along a surfaced single-track lane, passing a brick-built house on the right. Continue for 0.5 miles (800m), passing a right turning to Old Songhurst Farm.

4 Turn left on reaching a T-junction with a lane, following the Sussex Border Path, and pass Songhurst House. After 0.5 miles (800m), turn left at a T-junction opposite the Sir Roger Tichborne pub along the right-hand verge of the B2133. Soon turn right along Oakhurst Lane, following the Sussex Border Path towards Oakhurst Farm. Approaching the farm, leave the lane on the left through a gate, as signed, and follow the track which bypasses the farm, ignoring a footpath turn on the left. Beyond the barns, the track heads on into woodland. Keep ahead at the first T-junction, still following the Sussex Border Path. Carry on with a pond on your right to a crossing of tracks.

5 Turn left here and follow the Wey South Path alongside the disused Wey and Arun Junction Canal, which here appears as an overgrown ditch on the left. Continue on the old tow path, passing through several gates. Disregard any turnings and keep to the route of the canal. Pass the Southlands Lock and then the Devil's Hole Lock and Bridge. Nearing the B2133, follow the path under the road bridge back to the car park.

WHAT TO SEE In Spy Lane is the former chapel of a religious sect formed in the 19th century. The adjoining burial ground is the final resting place of founder John Sirgood and 600 of his followers, though there are no headstones to mark their graves. Sirgood was a puritanical evangelist who came to Loxwood in 1850. He gathered around him the Society of Dependents, whose members became known as Cokelers. The Cokelers carried out a great deal of charity work in the area, though they refused to solemnise marriage in their chapel, did not approve of music and books, and did not endorse sport or the theatre. The chapel is now home to the Emmanuel Fellowship, which has no connection with the extinct Cokelers.

WHILE YOU'RE THERE Enjoy a summer afternoon cruise on the restored section of the Wey and Arun Junction Canal. The weekend trips begin by the Onslow Arms in Loxwood and last less than an hour. Longer cruises on the canal take place once a month.

A Downland Ramble at Amberley

DISTANCE 4.5 miles (7.5km)   MINIMUM TIME 2hrs 30min

ASCENT/GRADIENT 525ft (160m) ▲▲▲   LEVEL OF DIFFICULTY ✦✦✦

PATHS Riverside paths, downland tracks and some roads, several stiles

LANDSCAPE Arun Valley and downland

SUGGESTED MAP AA Leisure Map 23 Brighton & The South Downs

START/FINISH Grid reference: TQ026118

DOG FRIENDLINESS Off lead on stretches of downland and riverside

PARKING Free parking at Amberley Station car park, or adjoining museum car park for visitors to the museum

PUBLIC TOILETS Amberley Working Museum

This invigorating downland walk begins where reality meets nostalgia. Visiting an old chalk quarry at the start of the route, you have the chance to forget, albeit briefly, the hurly-burly of the modern world, step into the past and recall a cherished way of life that has long vanished. Amberley is a charming, tranquil village with a history going back to medieval times, and was the summer residence of the Bishops of Chichester.

AMBERLEY WORKING MUSEUM

Amberley Working Museum is well worth a visit, entered via the Amberley railway station car park. The open-air museum, which covers 36 acres (15ha) originally of a long-disused chalk pit in the Arun Valley, was opened in 1979. Originally called the Chalk Pits Museum, its objective is to illustrate how the traditional industries of southeast England evolved and developed during the 19th and 20th centuries.

As well as changing its name in later years, the Amberley Museum also marketed itself as 'The Museum that Works'. And work it certainly does. Few museums thrill and excite adults and children alike as much as this one does. To prove it, there are almost 100,000 visitors a year.

GLIMPSES OF A PAST WORLD

Visit the bus garage and the signwriter's workshop, the locomotive shed, the village blacksmith's, stop at the telephone exchange or discover the wheelwright's shop. You may meet skilled craftspeople from the museum's resident team exercising ancient trades. Using traditional materials and tools, they produce a choice of fine wares which enables them to earn a living and keep their trade thriving. Elsewhere, exhibits

Left: An authentic old bus at the Amberley Working Museum (Walk 33)

are conserved and demonstrated by volunteers, many of whom have acquired a lifetime's experience in their trade.

One of the highlights of a visit to the Amberley Working Museum is a trip around the site on board a vintage bus, or perhaps a tour on the narrow-gauge railway. The train ride takes visitors between Amberley and Brockham stations, and yet never leaves the museum site. When you finally leave the museum, follow the River Arun and begin the gradual climb into the hills. Up here, with its wide-open skies and far-ranging views, you can feel the bracing wind in your face as you explore some of the loneliest tracts of downland anywhere in Sussex.

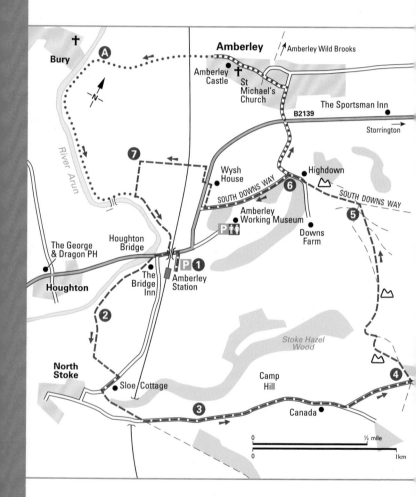

1 Turn left out of the car park and pass underneath the railway bridge. Begin to cross the road bridge spanning the Arun, bearing left at the footpath sign to reach a stile by a galvanised gate. After crossing a bridge and another stile, bear right on a riverside bank to the next stile. A few paces beyond this, reach a sluice. Bear left here.

2 Follow the path between trees, turn right on reaching a lane and pass Sloe Cottage. Turn left through a gate just beyond a caravan site to join a bridleway. Follow the path as it runs above the camping ground and emerge on a track by a bridleway sign. Cross the track here and join a rough lane, turning left.

3 Stay on the lane as it climbs gradually; the Arun can be seen below. Pass farm outbuildings and keep ahead, the lane dwindling to a track along this stretch. Veer left at the fork and follow the waymarked public right of way. Head for a signposted crossroads and turn left on a bridleway with a fence on your right.

4 Walk down the chalk track, pass through a gate and continue the steep descent. Look for two gates down below, set some distance apart. Cross to the right-hand gate; a bridleway sign should be nearby. Follow the bridleway as it bends left, climbing steeply towards Downs Farm. Keep a fence on the left and follow the bridleway, eventually merging with a wide track.

5 Keep left at the next junction and follow the South Downs Way towards the entrance to Downs Farm. Fork right at a junction, continuing on the South Downs Way, and join a narrow footpath which begins a steep descent. Drop down the slope until you reach a tarmac lane then turn right. On the right-hand side is a prominent house called Highdown.

6 Just beyond the house fork left, following the South Downs Way down the lane. The attractions of Amberley Working Museum can be spotted down to the left. Immediately before the road junction, turn right and follow the South Downs Way parallel to the road. Cross the main road, continue on the other side and turn left on a concrete track over the railway line, past the sewage works. The track turns left here in front of a metal gate and continues to the bank of the River Arun.

7 Leaving the South Downs Way, turn left along the riverbank path. Veering slightly left to pass behind the static caravans, join a drive and then turn left at the road. Bear right to return to the car park.

WHERE TO EAT AND DRINK The Bridge Inn at Houghton Bridge, close to the start of the walk, is Grade II listed and has fires and a welcoming atmosphere. Among the popular dishes are rump steak and steak and kidney pudding. Snacks include ploughmans' and sandwiches; also Sunday roasts and a children's menu. There is also a tea room at Houghton Bridge.

WHAT TO SEE A church at North Stoke, just off the route, is mentioned in the Domesday Book, though nothing here is earlier than the 13th century. The windows in both transepts have some of the most striking early tracery in southern England. From the higher ground, above North Stoke, look across the Arun Valley to the 'Alpine' spire of the church at South Stoke. On a good day you might pick out distant Arundel Castle.

WHILE YOU'RE THERE Take a look at the Arun by Houghton Bridge. This is a popular spot in the summer. A short distance away is the village of Houghton, which you might care to visit after the walk. The George and Dragon pub originally dates back to the 13th century; Charles II stopped here to take ale in October 1651, on his way to the coast after the Battle of Worcester.

Amberley Downs and Wild Brooks

DISTANCE 6 miles (9.7km)   MINIMUM TIME 3hrs

ASCENT/GRADIENT 525ft (160m) ▲▲▲   LEVEL OF DIFFICULTY ✦✦✦

SEE MAP AND INFORMATION PANEL FOR WALK 33

To extend Walk 34, veer right at the fork at Point ❻ and walk down to the B2139. Cross over the road into Amberley village and turn left just past the phone box and tea room. Continue along the road, passing St Michael's Church and Amberley Castle.

The castle dates back to Norman times and was strongly fortified in 1377. Originally it was the residence of the Bishops of Chichester. However, its fate was sealed when the Parliamentarians began to dismantle it during the Civil War. Parts of the castle survive today, having been converted into a stylish hotel. White peacocks and black swans inhabit the grounds and helicopters, ferrying guests, can sometimes be seen landing by the castle walls. The portcullis closes at midnight every night. Carry straight on.

Over to the right are glimpses of Amberley Wild Brooks, an extensive area of water-meadows that may seem to have more in common with the fenland of East Anglia than Sussex. These meadows have been designated a Site of Special Scientific Interest (SSSI) for their diversity of habitats – woodland, scrub and dry permanent pasture among them. You may spot Bewick swans and, if you're lucky, white-fronted geese. This is a popular haunt for wintering wildfowl.

Where the road ends beneath the castle wall, keep straight ahead on a path between fences. Cross two stiles, either side of the railway, and look for the spire of Bury church ahead. Follow the path to the next stile and cut across the field half-left towards a footpath sign. In the second field make for a stile and bridge ahead and cross the third field in the direction signposted to the riverbank and turn left, Point ❹. Follow the reed-fringed Arun. Avoid the distinctive metal footbridge and keep ahead with the river on the right to return to Houghton Bridge. Bear left for the museum car park.

WHERE TO EAT AND DRINK Situated half a mile east of Amberley village is The Sportsman, which in the past has been awarded both CAMRA country pub of the year and pub of the year for the Arun and Adur area. There are three bars and a conservatory restaurant boasting one of the best views in Sussex of the Amberley Wild Brooks. Traditional pub meals are served and real ales are predominantly from local breweries.

Right: Thatched cottage in Amberley village (Walks 33 and 34)

On Highdown Hill

DISTANCE 3.25 miles (5.3km)   MINIMUM TIME 1hr 30min

ASCENT/GRADIENT 82ft (25m) ▲▲▲   LEVEL OF DIFFICULTY +++

PATHS Grassy paths and well-defined bridleway

LANDSCAPE Breezy hilltop with good views over downland and coast

SUGGESTED MAP AA Leisure Map 23 Brighton & The South Downs

START/FINISH Grid reference: TQ098041

DOG FRIENDLINESS Highdown Hill is good for dog walking

PARKING Free car park and picnic area

PUBLIC TOILETS Highdown Gardens

Rising 266ft (81m) above the Sussex coast, Highdown Hill is a popular recreational area, a superb playground for children and a vital green lung on Worthing and Littlehampton's doorstep. Here you can enjoy a leisurely stroll, enhanced by a wonderful sense of space and distance.

HILL-FORT AND ITS HISTORY

Highdown is a site of considerable archaeological importance. Evidence of Bronze Age, Iron Age and Roman occupation has been found here, as well as one of the earliest Anglo-Saxon burial sites in England. The earliest permanent settlement was a Late Bronze Age (c.1000 BC) enclosure. This was followed in the early Iron Age (c.600 BC) by the construction of a hill-fort, composed of a single rampart and ditch. Subsequently the site was used as an Anglo-Saxon burial ground c.AD 450. It was discovered quite by accident in the late 19th century, when a local landowner was carrying out some tree planting inside the hill-fort. Excavations that followed between 1893 and 1894 uncovered 86 Anglo-Saxon graves. Most of the objects that were found, which include an unusual number of glass ones, are now on display in Worthing Museum.

In 1588 a beacon was lit here to warn of the approaching Spanish Armada and during World War II a radar station was built on the hill, causing considerable damage to the site during its construction. The great storm of 1987 caused further damage, uprooting many trees, and a rescue dig took place the following year.

Today Highdown is in the care of the National Trust. The Sompting Village Morris Dancers gather on the hill on 21 June to celebrate the summer solstice.

FLORA AND FAUNA

Highdown Hill's grassland includes a number of important wildlife habitats. Plants most closely associated with the old chalk grazing land include cowslip, kidney vetch, chalk milkwort and common spotted orchid. The carthusian snail, a rare mollusc, has been discovered here, and birds such as linnet, goldfinch and willow warbler are known to inhabit the area.

This short, airy walk combined with a visit to nearby Highdown Gardens provides a rewarding half day out. You might also like to call in at Highdown Vineyard, situated on the southern slope of the hill, and accessed from the A259, not far from the turn off to Highdown Hill. There's a shop and tea room, and wine tastings and tours can also be arranged.

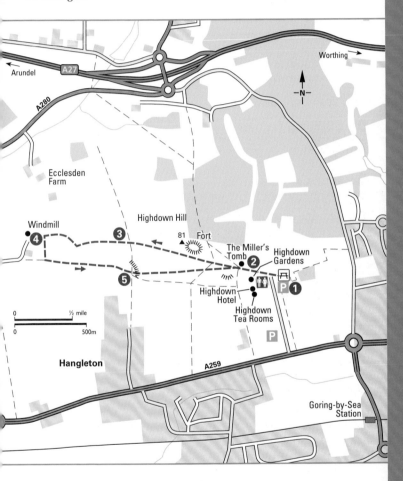

❶ With your back to the coast, follow the path from the top left-hand corner of the car park, immediately curving left. Keep ahead on the main path, passing a clump of bushes on your right, then veer right to the Miller's Tomb. Pass the tomb and go

through the gate to an interpretation board recording the fascinating history of Highdown Hill.

❷ Stride out along the top of the ridge over the hill, keeping the trees on your right. The remains of the hill-fort and its grassy earthworks can be seen now. To the right, at the western end of the site, you'll see a trig point.

❸ Descend gently to a gate and then go straight ahead in the next field. The stump of Ecclesden Windmill, minus its sails, can be seen in the distance. Soon the path curves to the right and hugs the field boundary, passing a track running off to the right. Maintain the same westerly direction and keep the field boundary on your right. Make for the field corner, turning left to follow the path between fences.

❹ The old windmill lies to your right now. Continue ahead to reach a junction with a bridleway. Turn left here and follow the path which leads between bushes and margins of vegetation. Eventually you reach a stile on the left. Disregard it, and no more than 10 paces beyond the stile you arrive at a junction of bridleways.

❺ Keep left here, and follow the track up the slope between the bushes. Very quickly you reach the exposed, lower slopes of Highdown Hill, following its contours in an easterly direction. Avoid the paths running up the hill and pass a fenced field on the right. Continue on the main path to reach a signpost. Keep ahead here towards the trees, rejoining the outward route at the interpretation board. Go through the gate, pass the Miller's Tomb and retrace your steps to the car park.

WHERE TO EAT AND DRINK Highdown Tea Rooms, open every day throughout the year, offers rolls, sandwiches, salads, ploughman's, cakes and cream teas. Next door is Highdown Hotel, which includes two bars, a family restaurant and a carvery restaurant. Light snacks, jacket potatoes and more substantial main courses are available, as is a children's menu.

WHAT TO SEE The Miller's Tomb contains the remains of John Oliver, an eccentric 18th-century miller, who, allegedly, had the tomb constructed on Highdown Hill more than 20 years before his death. The reason? So that smuggler Oliver could store contraband safely and in the least likely place. He died in 1793.

WHILE YOU'RE THERE Visit Highdown's lovely chalk garden, which is open throughout the year and was established by Sir Frederick and Lady Stern, who worked for 50 years to prove that plants would grow on chalk. The garden was created out of a disused chalk pit at a time when horticulturalists were travelling to China and the Himalayan regions to collect rare and beautiful plants. Many of the original species from those early expeditions survive in the garden today. Following Sir Frederick's death in 1967, his widow left the garden to Worthing Borough Council.

Climping – Where Countryside Meets Coast

DISTANCE 4 miles (6.4km)	MINIMUM TIME 2hrs

ASCENT/GRADIENT Negligible ▲▲▲   LEVEL OF DIFFICULTY ✚✚✚

PATHS Field paths, roads and stretches of beach

LANDSCAPE Sandy beaches, open farmland and riverside development

SUGGESTED MAP AA Walker's Map 20 Chichester & The South Downs

START/FINISH Grid reference: TQ005007

DOG FRIENDLINESS Off lead on enclosed paths and beach area. Under control near the Arun and on road at Climping

PARKING Car park at Climping Beach

PUBLIC TOILETS Climping Beach

Much of the Sussex coast has grown and evolved since early pioneering photographers captured classic seaside scenes at Worthing, Hove and Littlehampton, and now a chain of urban development extends almost continuously from Bognor to Brighton. Here and there are still hints of the coastline as it used to be before the builders moved in, but Climping Beach, where this walk begins, is an altogether different place. There is a welcome feeling of space and distance here, rarely experienced on the Sussex coast.

REMOTE SPOT

One of Climping's main attractions is its remoteness. It is approached along a country lane which terminates at the beach car park. A glance at a map of this area might cause some confusion. The village of Climping, which has a 13th-century church, lies a mile (1.6km) or so inland and the nearest settlement to Climping Beach is Atherington. The medieval church and various dwellings of this old parish now lie beneath the sea, which has steadily encroached upon the land, and all that is now left of low-lying Atherington are several houses and a hotel.

Climping Beach, together with neighbouring West Beach, is popular with holidaymakers as well as locals who want to enjoy the space. The National Trust protects more than 2 miles (3.2km) of coastline here. The low-water, sandy beach is backed by shingle banks which, in places, support vegetation, a rare habitat in Britain. In addition, there are active sand dunes, which are another rare and fragile feature of the coastline. Only six areas of active sand dunes survive on the south coast between Cornwall and Kent, and three of them are in Sussex.

After crossing a broad expanse of flat farmland, the walk eventually reaches the River Arun, opposite Littlehampton. From here it's a pleasant amble to West Beach, finishing with a spectacular stroll by the sea, back to Climping Beach. There is much to divert the attention along the way, but it is this lonely stretch of coastline that makes the greatest impression – a vivid reminder of how the entire West Sussex coast once looked.

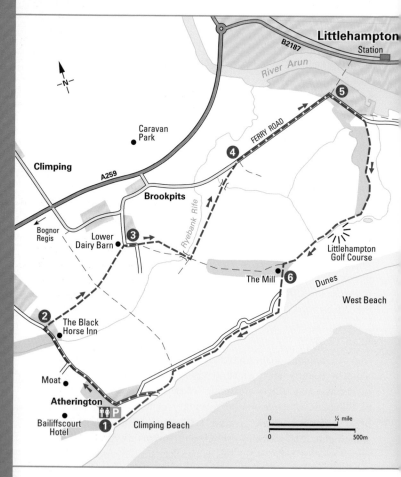

❶ From the beach car park take the road leading away from the sea, passing the entrance to Bailiffscourt Hotel on the left-hand side. Continue walking along the road until you reach The Black Horse Inn and take the next footpath on the right, by some thatched cottages.

❷ When the track swings left, continue ahead across the field to a signpost at a junction with a byway. Go straight over and follow the path through the fields towards a tile-roofed barn.

3 At the building, Lower Dairy Barn, join a track on a bend and turn right. As it swings right, take the signposted path and begin by following the boundary hedge. Stride out across the field, cross the concrete footbridge and bear left at the footpath sign to follow a deep ditch known as the Ryebank Rife. At a signpost, veer away from the ditch and cross the field to a line of trees, aiming towards a distant pale blue gasometer. Cross a footbridge to the road.

4 Turn right and walk along the pavement to a turning on the right for Littlehampton Golf Course. The walk follows this road, but first continue ahead for a few steps to have a look at the footbridge crossing the Arun. The buildings of Littlehampton can be seen on the far side and, if time allows, you may like to extend the walk by visiting the town.

5 Continuing the main walk, follow the road towards West Beach and the golf course, veering right at a car park sign to follow an enclosed path to a kissing gate at the corner of the golf course. Continuing ahead, the path (which can be very muddy) runs along a raised bank through trees and later emerges into the open with good views over this unspoilt coastal plain. Keep to the path and at the end of the golf course you reach a house known as The Mill. Avoid the path on the right here and keep left.

6 Continue walking along the footpath, which soon reaches West Beach. Look for the interpretation board which explains how this open stretch of coastline has been shaped and influenced by climatic conditions and the sea over the centuries. Follow the footpath ahead along the edge of the shingle beach (the road that runs parallel to it below is private) back to the car park. When the tide is out you can walk along the sand instead.

WHERE TO EAT AND DRINK The Black Horse Inn near Climping Beach is located on the route of the walk and is an ideal stop if you're completing it on a summer's evening. Eat and drink outside or relax in the cosy bar. The inn offers a range of ales and a wide selection of hot and cold food. Littlehampton has a good choice of pubs, including several in the vicinity of the Arun.

WHAT TO SEE As you begin the walk, look for the entrance to Bailiffscourt Hotel. Roger de Montgomery, William the Conqueror's cousin, permitted Benedictine monks from the Abbey of Seez to establish a chapel at Climping. Their bailiff occupied what is now the hotel. The building was later remodelled in the authentic medieval style.

WHILE YOU'RE THERE Read about the history of the bridge over the Arun. The river, which is fast-flowing and reaches up to 7 knots during the spring tides, effectively separates the town of Littlehampton from the adjoining countryside. The view downstream from the bridge is of various boatyards and Docklands-style warehouses which have been converted into apartments. Littlehampton was a thriving port during the Middle Ages, when stone from Normandy was landed here for the construction of many of the county's churches and castles. Later, it became a fashionable seaside resort with its seafront lined by striking Victorian and Edwardian villas.

Overleaf: Arundel Castle (Walk 37)

Castle and River at Arundel

DISTANCE 3.25 miles (5.3km)	MINIMUM TIME 2hrs

ASCENT/GRADIENT 197ft (60m) ▲▲▲   LEVEL OF DIFFICULTY ✦✦✦

PATHS Riverside and parkland paths, some road walking

LANDSCAPE Valley, rolling parkland and town

SUGGESTED MAP AA Walker's Map 20 Chichester & The South Downs

START/FINISH Grid reference: TQ020071

DOG FRIENDLINESS Off lead on tow path. Not permitted in Arundel Park. Final stage of the walk is along busy roads in Arundel

PARKING Mill Road fee-paying car park, Arundel

PUBLIC TOILETS Near to car park in Mill Road; Swanbourne Lake

NOTES Arundel Park is closed annually on 24 March

Arundel has rows of elegant Georgian and Victorian buildings, fine shops and a picturesque riverside setting, but topping the list of attractions is surely the town's magnificent castle – the jewel in Arundel's crown. As you drive along the A27 to the south of Arundel, the great battlemented castle, together with the grandiose French Gothic-style Roman Catholic cathedral, can be seen standing guard over the town, dwarfing all the other buildings in sight.

NORFOLK HOUSE

There has been a castle here since the 11th century, though most of the present fortification is Victorian. Arundel Castle is the principal ancestral home of the Dukes of Norfolk, formerly the Earls of Arundel. There are various family portraits inside the castle, some of them believed to date back to the Wars of the Roses. The Norfolks have lived at Arundel since the 16th century. According to the plaque at the bottom of the High Street: 'Since William Rose and Harold fell, There have been Earls at Arundel'.

The castle was attacked by Parliamentary forces during the Civil War, and was rebuilt and restored in the 18th and 19th centuries. Within its great walls lies a treasure trove of sumptuous riches, including a fascinating collection of fine furniture dating from the 16th century, tapestries, clocks and portraits by Van Dyck, Gainsborough, Reynolds, Mytens and Lawrence – among others. Personal items belonging to Mary, Queen of Scots and an assortment of religious and heraldic items from the Duke of Norfolk's collection can also be viewed.

The walk starts down by the Arun and from here there are teasing glimpses of the castle, but it is not until you have virtually finished the walk that you reach its main entrance, saving the best until last. Following the riverbank through the tranquil Arun valley, renowned for its bird life, the walk eventually reaches Arundel Park, a delight in any season. Swanbourne Lake, a great attraction for young children, lies by the entrance to the park, making it easily accessible for everyone. However, once the bustling lake scene fades from view and the sound of children at play finally dies, the park assumes a totally different character. Rolling hills and tree-clad slopes crowd in from every direction and only occasional serious walkers, some of them following the long-distance Monarch's Way recreational path, are likely to be seen in these more remote surroundings.

You may feel isolated at this point, but the interlude is soon over when you find yourself back in Arundel. Pass the huge edifice of the cathedral, built in 1870, and make your way down to the castle entrance. Walk down the High Street, said to be the steepest in England, and by the bridge at the bottom you can see the remains of the Blackfriars monastery, dissolved in 1546 by Henry VIII.

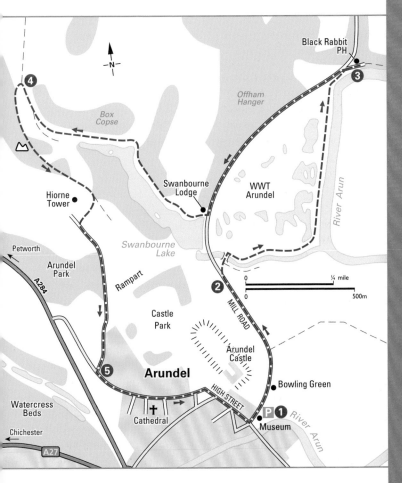

1 From the car park in Mill Road, turn right and walk along the tree-lined pavement. Pass the bowling green and a glance to your left will reveal a dramatic view of Arundel Castle with its imposing battlements.

2 Follow the road to the elegant stone bridge, avoid the first path on the right and cross over via a footbridge, and turn right to join the riverside path, partly shaded by overhanging trees. Continue along this, emerging from the trees to reach the western bank of the Arun. Turn left here and walk beside the reed-fringed Arun to the Black Rabbit pub, which can be seen standing out against a curtain of trees.

3 From the Black Rabbit, turn left on the minor road back towards Arundel, passing the entrance to the WWT Arundel Wetland Centre. About 300 yards beyond the Centre pass through a gate on the right leading into Arundel Park past Swanbourne Lodge and follow the path alongside Swanbourne Lake. Eventually the lake fades from view as the walk reaches deeper into the park. Ignore a turning branching off to the left, just before a gate and stile, and follow the path as it curves gently to the right.

4 Turn sharply to the left at the next waymarked junction and begin a fairly steep ascent, with the footpath through the park seen curving away down to the left, back towards the lake. This stretch of the walk offers glorious views over elegant Arundel Park. Head for a stile and gate, then bear immediately right up the bank. Cross the grass, following the waymarks and keeping to the left of Hiorne Tower. On reaching a driveway, turn left and walk down to Park Lodge. Keep to the right by the private drive and make for the road.

5 Turn left, pass Arundel Cathedral and bear left at the road junction by the entrance to Arundel Castle. Go down the hill, back into the centre of Arundel. You'll find Mill Road at the bottom of the High Street.

WHERE TO EAT AND DRINK Arundel offers a good choice of places to eat and drink. The Black Rabbit at Offham, on the route of the walk, is delightfully situated on the Arun. Cheerful hanging baskets add plenty of colour in summer when you can sit outside and relax in attractive surroundings. The WWT Arundel Wetland Centre has a cafe by the water's edge and there are tea rooms at Swanbourne Lodge serving cream teas and a variety of cakes.

WHAT TO SEE Climbing up from Arundel Park brings you to Hiorne Tower, a remote but beautifully situated folly. Triangular in plan and recently restored, the folly was built by Francis Hiorne in an effort to ingratiate himself with the then Duke of Norfolk so that he might work on the restoration of Arundel Castle. The duke agreed to engage him on the restoration but Hiorne died before he could begin work.

WHILE YOU'RE THERE Visit the Wildfowl and Wetlands Trust Conservation Centre, which is situated directly on the route of the walk. There are many attractions to divert your attention. Ducks, geese and swans from all over the world make their home here and the popular boardwalk enables you to explore one of the largest reed beds in Sussex. Arundel's new, purpose-built museum, situated next door to the car park in Mill Road, features displays about the castle, town and river.

Exploring the Slindon Estate

DISTANCE 4 miles (6.4km)   MINIMUM TIME 2hrs

ASCENT/GRADIENT 82ft (25m) ▲▲▲   LEVEL OF DIFFICULTY ✦✦✦

PATHS Woodland, downland paths and tracks

LANDSCAPE Sweeping downland and woodland

SUGGESTED MAP AA Walker's Map 20 Chichester & The South Downs

START/FINISH Grid reference: SU960076

DOG FRIENDLINESS Unless signed otherwise, off lead, except in Slindon village

PARKING Free National Trust car park in Park Lane, Slindon

PUBLIC TOILETS None on route

In 1895 the National Trust was founded by three far-sighted, visionary Victorians whose objective was to acquire sites of historic interest and natural beauty for the benefit of the nation.

TRUST IN FUTURE GENERATIONS

The Trust has come a long way since those early, pioneering days. More than 100 years after its foundation, it is the country's biggest landowner, depending on donations and legacies and the annual subscriptions of its two million members for much of its income. The statistics are awesome. Over the years it has acquired 600,000 acres (243,000ha) of countryside, much of which is freely open to everyone, 550 miles (891km) of coastline, over 300 historic houses and more than 150 gardens, all of which it aims to preserve and protect for future generations. It is some achievement.

SLINDON ESTATE

Much of the West Sussex village of Slindon is part of the National Trust's 3,500-acre (1,419ha) Slindon Estate, which is situated on the southern slopes of the South Downs between Arundel and Chichester. The estate, the setting for this lovely walk, was originally designed and developed as an integrated community and it is the Trust's aim to maintain this structure as far as possible.

Take a stroll through Slindon village as you end the walk and you can see that many of the cottages are built of brick and flint, materials typical of chalk country. During the medieval period, long before the National Trust was established, Slindon was an important estate of the Archbishops of Canterbury. Earlier still it was home to Neolithic people who settled at Barkhale, a hilltop site at its northern end.

As well as the village, the estate consists of a large expanse of sweeping downland dissected by dry valleys, a folly, several farms and a stretch of Roman road. Glorious hanging beechwoods on the scarp enhance the picture, attracting walkers and naturalists in search of peace and solitude. Parts of the estate were damaged in the storms of 1987 and 1990, though the woods are regenerating, with saplings and woodland plants flourishing in the lighter glades. Typical ground plants of the beechwoods include bluebell, dog's mercury, greater butterfly orchid and wood sedge.

To help celebrate its centenary in 1995, the National Trust chose the Slindon Estate to launch its 100 Paths Project, a scheme designed to enhance access to its countryside properties by creating or improving paths. This unspoiled landscape offers many miles of footpaths and bridleways for a country walk.

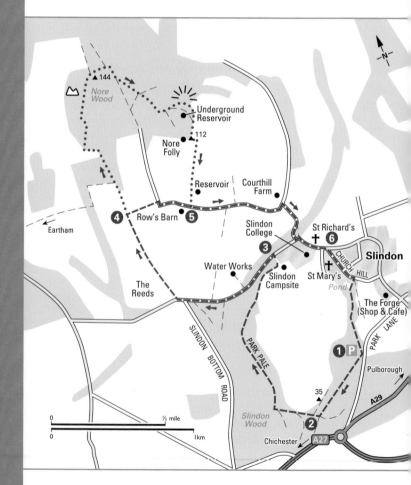

1 From the car park walk towards the road and turn right, passing through the gate to join a wide straight path cutting between trees and bracken. The path runs alongside sunny glades and clearings and between lines of attractive beech and silver birch trees before reaching a crossroads.

2 Turn right to a second crossroads and continue ahead here, keeping the grassy bank and ditch (all that remains of the Park Pale) on your right. Follow the broad path as it begins a wide curve to the right – the boundary ditch is still visible here running parallel to the path. On reaching a kissing gate, continue ahead, soon skirting fields. As you approach the entrance to Slindon campsite, swing left and follow the track down to the road.

3 Turn left and follow the road through the woodland. Pass Slindon Bottom Road and turn right after a few paces to join a bridleway. Follow the path as it cuts between fields and look for a path on the right.

4 Cross the stile, go down the field and up the other side, and join a track. Turn right and follow it as it immediately bends left. Walk along to Row's Barn and continue ahead on the track. Nore Folly can be seen over to the left.

5 Continue straight ahead along the track, following it gently down. Pass Courthill Farm on the left and turn right at the road. Follow the lane, or soon branch left on to a parallel woodland path to the next road. Bear left and pass Slindon College on the right and St Richard's Catholic Church on the left before reaching Church Hill.

6 Fork right into Church Hill, pass the church and make for the pond, a weeping willow reaching down to the water's edge. Look for mallard ducks here. Turn right around the far end of the pond on the obvious waterside path to enter the wood. On reaching a fork, by a National Trust sign for the Slindon Estate, keep left and walk ahead through the trees, ignoring any side paths, to return to the car park.

WHERE TO EAT AND DRINK The George at Eartham (off the route by 0.75 miles/1.2km) serves traditional pub food as well as seasonal dishes using local produce. The bar and dining room are open plan and there is a secluded beer garden. The historic old village forge at Slindon has a shop and cafe, offering light lunches and afternoon teas.

WHAT TO SEE As you stroll through peaceful Slindon Wood look for the remains of the medieval Park Pale, more commonly described as a bank and ditch. This was originally designed to protect the park's deer. In Palaeolithic times, the sea extended this far inland – hard to believe now as you look at the wooded surroundings. A preserved shingle beach indicates that the sea was once 130ft (40m) higher than it is today. Courthill Farm, towards the end of the walk, was once the home of the French-born writer Hilaire Belloc and his wife when they were first married. He spent part of his childhood in the village.

WHILE YOU'RE THERE Have a look at the church of St Mary, which is partly Norman and greatly restored. Inside is a rare wooden effigy to Sir Anthony St Leger who died in 1539. Slindon House, now part of a college, was one of the rest-houses of the Archbishops of Canterbury during the Middle Ages.

Slindon Estate and Out to Nore Folly

DISTANCE 5.75 miles (9.3km)   MINIMUM TIME 2hrs 45min

ASCENT/GRADIENT 210ft (64m) ▲▲▲   LEVEL OF DIFFICULTY ✚✚✚

PATHS Hanging beechwoods and remote downland, several stiles

SEE MAP AND INFORMATION PANEL FOR WALK 38

It's well worth extending Walk 38 if you've got the time. The woodland stretches, through glorious beechwoods, are deliciously cool on a baking hot summer day and the views throughout the walk over rural Sussex are really outstanding.

Don't turn right at the stile at Point ❹; instead go straight on along the bridleway, heading north. Ignore a turning for Eartham on the left, pass a bridleway sign and follow the path as it begins to climb quite steeply between the trees. On the higher ground the bridleway starts to widen, picking its way through extensive woodland.

Descend to a junction with a bridleway and turn right following the yellow arrow. 100yds (91m) later fork left through a wooden barrier. Continue through the woodland to a junction, with the boundaries of an underground reservoir partly visible on the right. Go forward through a galvanised gate and, as you emerge from the extensive tree cover, you

may want to stop for a moment to enjoy the breathtaking view of the coast, including the white tent-like structure of Butlins at Bognor Regis and, to the right, the Isle of Wight and Chichester Cathedral. Walk ahead, following the track down to the trig point.

Previously seen from a distance, Nore Folly suddenly looms large beside you. Built for the Countess of Newburgh, reputedly as a copy of an Italian archway she had seen in a print, the 18th-century folly was later enlarged for use as a shooting lodge. The National Trust carried out extensive repair work in 1973 and today the brick and flint archway still stands.

Turn left here and then right along the edge of the field, the path parallel to the stony track on the other side of the hedge. The path is enclosed by hedges some of the way down. On reaching a track turn left, rejoining Walk 38 to follow Points ❺ and ❻ returning to the car park.

Around Bignor's Roman Remains

DISTANCE 5.25 miles (8.5km)   MINIMUM TIME 2hrs

ASCENT/GRADIENT 773ft (236m) ▲▲▲   LEVEL OF DIFFICULTY ✦✦✦

PATHS Downland and woodland tracks and paths, country roads

LANDSCAPE Rolling countryside and well-wooded slopes

SUGGESTED MAP AA Walker's Map 20 Chichester & The South Downs

START/FINISH Grid reference: SU974129

DOG FRIENDLINESS Quiet lanes with little traffic. Parts of walk follow tracks and paths where dogs can run free

PARKING Bignor Hill free car park

PUBLIC TOILETS Bignor Villa – open March to October

NOTES Before setting off on this walk it's worth walking up to the top of nearby Bignor Hill (c.1 mile/1.6km there and back) to enjoy the views

Bignor is most famous for its Roman villa situated just outside the village, a vineyard planted on the slopes below. From here the eye is drawn south towards the northern escarpment of the South Downs and Bignor Hill, which rises to 738ft (225m). From this lofty vantage point there are excellent views east along the length of the Downs towards the Arun valley and beyond. In spring and summer the grassland around here is full of wild flowers and butterflies.

Bignor Hill is part of the National Trust's 1,400 hectare Slindon Estate. Also part of the estate is Gumber Farm, to the southwest, which during World War II was used as a decoy airfield, using lights at night and wooden aeroplanes during the day to mimic a military airfield and thus attempt to protect the real airfields at Ford and Tangmere from being bombed. Today it is a working sheep farm.

BIGNOR ROMAN VILLA

The Roman Villa at Bignor is one of the largest in Britain. Discovered by a ploughman in 1811, Bignor features various mosaics which are considered to be among the finest in the country, depicting scenes of gladiators and representations of Venus and Medusa. Originally the villa consisted of about 70 buildings situated in a walled enclosure of over 4 acres (1.6ha). The entire estate may have extended to about 200 acres (81ha), confirming that a wealthy or influential person would have lived here, possibly the equivalent of a modern aristocrat. Construction of the building was probably started around the end of the 2nd century AD and it may well have been occupied for at least 200 years.

The Grade I listed Holy Cross Church in Bignor village largely dates to the 13th century, though a notable feature is the 11th-century Norman arch dividing the nave and chancel. The font is also Norman. The church is used on a regular basis; its 'Weed Festival' is quite renowned, with the church transformed using great quantities of locally grown weeds and wild flowers.

Dating from 1420 and Grade II listed, the Yeoman's House – passed on the walk – is a superb example of a medieval hall house, probably the best-preserved building of its type in England.

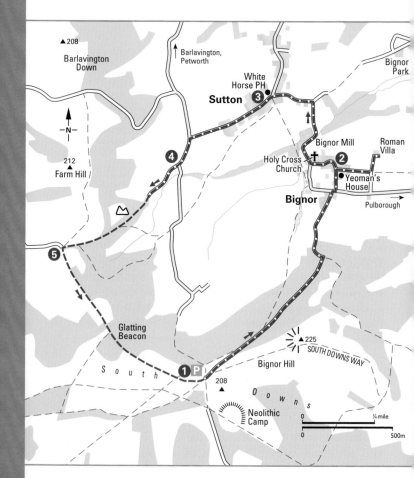

❶ From the car park, where there's a large wooden signpost and information board, follow the tarmac lane down towards Bignor Roman Villa. There are classic views between the trees over extensive Sussex landscape. The lane descends through the woodland, passing a

bridleway on the right as it bends left. On reaching Bignor village, pass a farm and bear briefly right and then left to take the road ahead signposted 'Sutton and Duncton'. Pass a telephone box and on the right is the picturesque Yeoman's House. To visit the Roman Villa, turn right along the access road here, continuing along a footpath. On reaching the drive turn left to the entrance.

2 Retrace your steps to the Yeoman's House and continue ahead along the road. The road bends left and passes the Parish Church of the Holy Cross. A yew tree, so familiar to country churchyards, can be seen in the corner. Follow the lane, ignoring a left turn, as it descends steeply through the trees and then climbs between high hedges towards Sutton. Pass the village sign and follow the road as it bends left by a bridleway running off to the right. Walk into the village.

3 When the road bends right by the White Horse, go straight on towards Barlavington and Duncton. Follow the lane between stone-built houses and cottages and head out of the village. Keep left at the fork and follow the 'No through road'. A tree-clad scarp, the walk's next objective, looms ahead.

4 As the lane bends left, fork right on the bridleway. Further on, the track

can become wet and muddy at the point where you share the route with a stream. You reach drier ground soon enough. Begin a gentle, slow ascent through the woodland and gradually the path narrows and becomes progressively steeper. The dramatic ascent eases further up and here you avoid a left-hand footpath. Soon daylight can be seen ahead, reaching through the trees.

5 At a meeting point of tracks, go forward and then bear left after about 30yds (27m). Follow the chalk track as it climbs gently, with far-ranging views over remote, well-wooded country. The track curves towards two masts on Glatting Beacon which can be seen peeping above the trees. Pass a National Trust sign for Bignor Hill and a bridleway on the right. Keep forward through woodland and now the track begins a gentle descent. Gradually the views widen to reveal glorious woodland and downland stretching into the distance. Head down to a junction, keep ahead on the South Downs Way and follow it back to the car park.

WHERE TO EAT AND DRINK Bignor Roman Villa includes a free picnic area for visitors and a cafeteria providing tea, coffee and light snacks. The White Horse pub at Sutton lies at the foot of the South Downs, directly on the route of the walk. There is a good choice of imaginative food and a selection of popular beers.

WHAT TO SEE Near the end of the walk is a charming dew pond, one of a number to be found on the South Downs. Originally used for watering sheep before there was piped water and troughs, these traditional ponds are important wildlife habitats as well as a classic feature of the landscape. Dew ponds owe their name to folklore; the vast majority of the water that fills them comes from rainfall.

WHILE YOU'RE THERE Pause to appreciate the landscape and history of the South Downs near Bignor. There is strong evidence of the Roman occupation here and running across Bignor Hill is Stane Street, a Roman road constructed about AD 70 to connect the port of Chichester (Noviomagus) with London (Londinium), a distance of some 56 miles (90km). You pass a section of the road at the end of the walk when you join the South Downs Way. The raised bank ('agger') you see marks the route of the old road.

A Walk at Glorious Goodwood

DISTANCE 3.5 miles (5.7km)   MINIMUM TIME 1hr 30min

ASCENT/GRADIENT 328ft (100m) ▲▲▲   LEVEL OF DIFFICULTY ✚✚✚

PATHS Woodland tracks and field paths, section of Monarch's Way and one lengthy stretch of quiet road

LANDSCAPE Mixture of dense woodland and scenic downland

SUGGESTED MAP AA Walker's Map 20 Chichester & The South Downs

START/FINISH Grid reference: SU898113

DOG FRIENDLINESS Can run free on woodland tracks

PARKING Counter's Gate free car park and picnic area at Goodwood Country Park

PUBLIC TOILETS Weald and Downland Open Air Museum

Think of horse racing on the South Downs and you immediately think of Goodwood, one of Britain's loveliest and most famous racecourses. The course rises and falls around a natural amphitheatre, with the horses dashing along the ridge to create one of the greatest spectacles in the racing world. Its superb position amid magnificent beechwoods high on the Downs draws crowds from far and wide, and for one week every summer thousands of racegoers attend one of the most prestigious events of the sporting and social calendar, 'Glorious Goodwood'. According to *The Times*, Goodwood is 'the place to be and to be seen'.

UNFORTUNATE REPUTATION

The course opened in 1801 after the Duke of Richmond gave part of his estate, Goodwood Park, to establish a track where members of the Goodwood Hunt Club and officers of the Sussex Militia could attend meetings. Towards the end of the 19th century the racecourse acquired a rather unfortunate reputation in the area when the rector of nearby Singleton protested to the Chief Constable in the strongest terms over the rowdy behaviour of racegoers. As a result, the crowds were restrained.

HUNT WITH TRADITION

The walk begins at Goodwood Country Park, a popular amenity area characterised by woodland and downland grass, and initially follows part of the Monarch's Way through extensive woodland and down to the village of East Dean. Along the road is neighbouring Charlton, famous for the Charlton Hunt. Established in the 18th century, the hunt's most memorable chase took place on 28th January 1738, beginning before eight that morning and not finishing until nearly six that evening. Many of those taking part were from the elite, upper ranks of society and for ten hours that day a fox led the pack a merry dance in the surrounding fields and woods. Eventually, the hounds cornered their prey, an elderly vixen, near the River Arun.

If time allows, you may want to extend the walk at this point and visit the Weald and Downland Museum, with its unusual collection of traditional homes and workplaces in both village and countryside. The main walk finishes by skirting Goodwood and on race days crowds line the bridleway alongside it, watching as camera crews dash back and forth in an effort to capture the best television images.

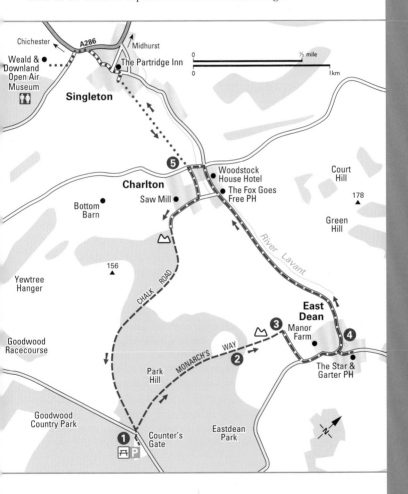

1 Make for the western end of Counter's Gate car park and look for a footpath sign by an opening leading out to the road. Cross over to a junction of two clear

tracks, with a path on the right. Follow the right-hand track, which is signposted 'public footpath', and is part of the Monarch's Way, to a gate and stile. Continue to the next gate and stile and then cross a clearing in the woods.

❷ Cut through this remote, thickly wooded country, following the gently curving path over the grassy, plant-strewn ground and down between trees to reach a gateway. The village of East Dean can be seen nestling down below. Head diagonally right down the steep field slope to reach a stile in the corner.

❸ Cross into the adjacent field and follow the boundary to a second stile leading out to the road. Bear left and walk down into East Dean, passing Manor Farm. Keep right at the junction in the village centre and, if it's opening time, follow the road towards Petworth in order to visit The Star & Garter pub.

❹ Leave East Dean by keeping the pond on your right-hand side and follow the road towards Midhurst and Singleton. On reaching Charlton village, pass The Fox Goes Free pub and the Woodstock House Hotel and take the next left turning. Follow the lane to a stile on the right and a

turning on the left. (To visit the Open Air Museum at Singleton, cross over into the fields and follow the straight path. At the end of the field bear right then left to a residential road. Keep straight ahead and then continue along a walkway between houses. You'll reach a green and playground with the church beyond. Turn right from the church car park to the road, left past The Partridge Inn, left at the main road and left again. The museum is just up this road on the right. Return to this stile by the same route and take the road opposite.)

❺ Walk along to the junction and turn right by the war memorial, dedicated to fallen comrades of the Sussex Yeomanry in both World Wars. Follow the track (Chalk Road) past houses and then on up through the trees. On the left are glimpses of a glorious rolling landscape, while to the right Goodwood's superb downland racecourse edges into view between the trees. Stay on the track all the way to the road and cross over to return to the Counter's Gate car park.

WHERE TO EAT AND DRINK The Star & Garter at East Dean and the 400-year-old The Fox Goes Free at Charlton both offer a good range of meals and snacks and enjoy a very pleasant South Downs setting. There is a cafe at the Weald and Downland Open Air Museum, offering hot soup, filled rolls, quiche, Cornish pasties and various cakes and pastries made with flour from the local working watermill.

WHAT TO SEE The village of East Dean, with its pond and ancient cottages of Sussex flint, is one of the prettiest in the area. For many years it was a thriving centre for hurdlemaking, and before World War I seven craftsmen operated here.

WHILE YOU'RE THERE Visit the Weald and Downland Open Air Museum which includes many attractions. Set in 50 acres (20ha) of lovely Sussex countryside, the museum offers a fascinating collection of some 50 regional historic buildings which have been saved from destruction, painstakingly restored and rebuilt in their original form. You can discover Victorian labourers' cottages, visit a recreated Tudor farmstead and tour the remarkable, prizewinning Downland Gridshell.

Meandering Around Midhurst

DISTANCE 3 miles (4.8km)   MINIMUM TIME 2hrs

ASCENT/GRADIENT 123ft (37m) ▲▲▲   LEVEL OF DIFFICULTY ✦✦✦

PATHS Pavements, field, riverside tracks and country road

LANDSCAPE Midhurst town and its beautiful rural setting on the Rother

SUGGESTED MAP AA Walker's Map 20 Chichester & The South Downs

START/FINISH Grid reference: SU887217

DOG FRIENDLINESS Off lead on tracks and stretches of riverside. On lead on roads and busy streets in Midhurst town centre

PARKING Car park by tourist information centre in North Street

PUBLIC TOILETS Car park

Midhurst is a classic Sussex town crying out to be discovered and explored on foot. Many splendid buildings and a wealth of history add to its charm and character. HG Wells attended school at Midhurst and wrote: 'I found something very agreeable and picturesque in its clean and cobbled streets, its odd turnings and abrupt corners, and in the pleasant park that crowds up one side of the town'. Midhurst became the model for Wimblehurst in his book *Tono Bungay*.

ESTATE YELLOW

Look around you on this walk and you'll spot the vivid yellow paintwork of houses owned by the Cowdray Estate. The grounds of Cowdray Park are famous for polo matches. Not so well known are the majestic ruins of Cowdray House, seen from the car park at the start of the walk and viewed up close just before you finish it. The house, built for the Earl of Southampton, dates back to about 1530 but was largely destroyed by fire in 1793. However, the shell survives and, if open, you can see around the Great Chamber, the Great Parlour and the Chapel.

Begin the walk with an easy stroll through the old market town of Midhurst with plenty to see along the way. Photographs of the town taken in the early part of the 20th century show the part-16th-century Angel Hotel and the building which now houses Barclays Bank. The famous tile-hung library has been preserved too, and the medieval interior is certainly worth looking at. Built in the early part of the 16th century, the building was thought originally to have been a storehouse or granary. This part of Midhurst is known as Knockhundred Row. The name is thought to date back to the time when Midhurst had a castle, and the owner could exercise his right to summon 100 men to defend the castle by knocking on the doors of 100 households in the town.

The road passes the old chemist shop where HG Wells worked before attending Midhurst Grammar School. His mother was housekeeper at nearby Uppark House. In the middle of the street, flanked by striking houses and shop fronts, lies the town's war memorial on which the names of several regiments are recorded. Follow the road to the imposing Parish Church of St Mary Magdalen and St Denys, which is mostly 19th century but with earlier traces.

The walk leaves Midhurst and heads for rolling, wooded countryside, eventually following a path running through woodland above the Rother. Here you can step between the trees on the right to look down at the river and across to Cowdray House. This vista is one of the highlights of the walk, which finishes by following the Queen's Path, a favourite walk of Elizabeth I.

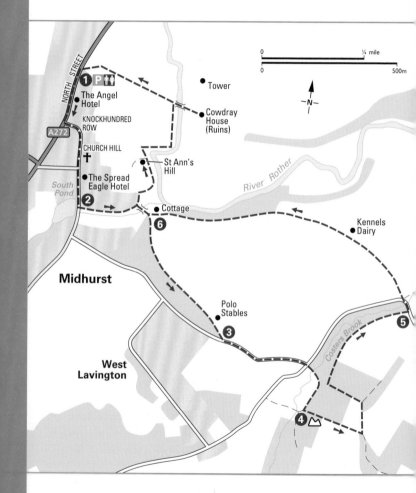

❶ From the car park by the tourist information centre turn left along North Street, passing the post office.

Bear left into Knockhundred Row; the road bends right and becomes Church Hill. When it splits (one-way traffic) keep left, passing the war memorial on your right and the church on your left. Continue into South Street past the historic The Spread Eagle Hotel.

2 Turn left by South Pond into The Wharf, following a bridleway beside industrial buildings and flats. Trees on the right enclose a stream. Bear right at the next waymarked junction, cross the bridge and pass a cottage on the left. Keep the wooden fencing on the right and avoid the path running off to the left. Go through a kissing gate, then continue ahead along the edge of fields, keeping trees and vegetation on the right. Go through another kissing gate and follow the path to the right of the polo stables.

3 Keep left and follow a wooded stretch of road. Pass some pretty cottages, and on reaching a bend keep ahead along a bridle path signposted 'Heyshott and Graffham'. Follow the track as it curves to the right.

4 Veer left at a fingerpost just before the entrance to a house and follow the waymarked path as it climbs quite steeply through the trees, passing between woodland glades and carpets of bracken. Drop down the slope to

a waymarked path junction and turn left to join a sandy track. Keep left at the fork and follow the track as it bends sharply to the right.

5 On reaching the road, turn left and, when it bends left by some gates, go straight on along the bridleway towards Kennels Dairy. Keep to the left of the outbuildings and stable blocks and carry on ahead to a gate. Continue on the path and, when it reaches a field gateway, go through the gate to the right of it, following the path as it runs just inside the woodland.

6 Continue along to the junction, forming part of the outward leg of the walk, turn right and cross the bridge. Keep ahead past the access road/ bridleway on the left (your outward route), then bear right to rejoin the riverbank. Keep going until you reach a footpath on the left leading up to the ruins of St Ann's Hill. Follow the path beside the Rother, curving right. Continue to a kissing gate, turn left and carry on to a bridge which provides access to Cowdray House. After viewing the house, go straight ahead along the causeway path to the car park.

WHERE TO EAT AND DRINK Midhurst has several pubs and hotels – among them The Angel in North Street. This extended Tudor coaching inn has a brasserie, set lunches through the week and light snacks in the more informal surroundings of the bar. The Coffee Pot in Knockhundred Row and Ye Olde Tea Shoppe in North Street offer tea, coffee and lunches.

WHAT TO SEE South Pond is one of Midhurst's most popular attractions. Donated to the town by Lord Cowdray in 1957, the pond is part of a tributary of the Rother. Mute swans, Canada geese and mallards can be seen here. A path running alongside South Pond was opened in 1977 to mark the Queen's Silver Jubilee.

WHILE YOU'RE THERE Have a look at St Ann's Hill, just off the route of the walk, above the River Rother. This natural mound was once the site of a fortified Norman castle, though all that remains of it today are a few stones amid this grassy knoll.

Tennyson's Black Down

DISTANCE 4.5 miles (7.2km)   MINIMUM TIME 2hrs

ASCENT/GRADIENT 315ft (96m) ▲▲▲   LEVEL OF DIFFICULTY +++

PATHS Woodland paths and tracks, some minor roads

LANDSCAPE Wooded hills on Sussex/Surrey Border

SUGGESTED MAP AA Walker's Map 23 Guildford, Farnham & The Downs

START/FINISH Grid reference: SU922306

DOG FRIENDLINESS Off lead away from car park and roads

PARKING Free car park off Tennyson's Lane (by National Trust sign for Blackdown), near Aldworth House to the southeast of Haslemere

PUBLIC TOILETS None on route

Situated close to the Sussex border with Surrey, Black Down lies in some of the loveliest countryside in southern England. At 919ft (280m), this prominent, pine-clad summit is the highest point in the county, yet for some reason it has never achieved the popular status of other high Sussex landmarks such as Devil's Dyke, Ditchling Beacon or Ashdown Forest. Part of a plateau of nearly 500 acres (202ha), Black Down is owned and cared for by the National Trust.

BIRDS AND BEES

It was the Victorians who made it a popular local destination for walkers and naturalists. Writers and artists loved it too, and parts of Black Down remain much the same now as they were around the end of the 19th century when young ladies walked here in groups, the botanists among them admiring the plants and wild flowers.

One man in particular gave Black Down his personal stamp of approval – Alfred, Lord Tennyson. The Poet Laureate built his second home here in 1868, living at Aldworth House for the last 24 years of his life. Ever the patriot, it is said he laid the foundation stone for his new home on 23 April – St George's Day and William Shakespeare's birthday. Tennyson was greatly inspired by the beauty and solitude of the area, writing these words in 'Lines to a Friend':

> You came, and look'd, and loved the view
> Long known and loved by me,
> Green Sussex fading into blue
> With one grey glimpse of sea.

DARK LANDSCAPE

Black Down is part of the range of sandstone hills which is enclosed by the bowl-shaped perimeter of the North and South Downs. Historic artefacts found in this area indicate there was human activity here as early as the middle Stone Age, 6000 BC. The name comes from the firs which rise out of a dark, heathery landscape, and not from the iron industry which once flourished around here.

Some of the most ancient tracks in Sussex cut across this hill, and the area was once a haunt of smugglers who may have used a cave here to hide their contraband, en route to London from the south coast.

BEACON SITE

Not surprisingly, Black Down was chosen as a beacon site, one of a chain to warn London of the threat of invasion on the south coast. The coming of the Spanish Armada in July 1588 was relayed via the beacon here, which would have been lit on a position high up, overlooking the Sussex Weald. This superb walk explores Black Down and its hidden corners. Not only does it guide you to one of the loveliest viewpoints in Sussex, but it allows you to picture its most distinguished resident, Alfred, Lord Tennyson, strolling this glorious plateau.

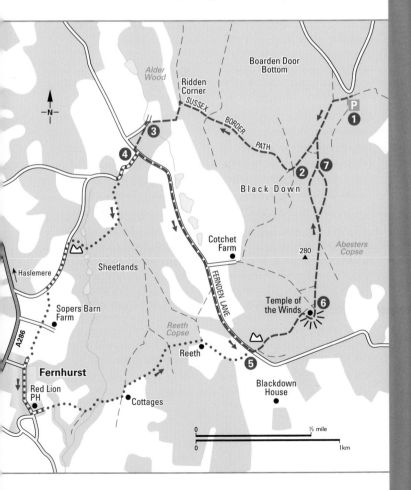

1 Turn left out of the car park and immediately left again on a rising path to the right of the National Trust sign. Keep left at the junction, then bear right at the fork and keep right just after a pond, also right, on the Sussex Border Path and Serpent Trail.

2 Turn right at a complex junction of paths. Keep left at the fork, still on the Sussex Border Path, and pass over a crossroads and through a gate. Veer left just beyond it at the fork and drop down to some rhododendron bushes. Turn sharp left here through a gate and follow the path through a tunnel of trees.

3 Bear left at a drive by a house and when, after a few paces, it curves right, go straight on to the right of a pond through the trees to join the road.

4 Turn left towards the entrance to Sheetlands. Avoid the turning and follow the lane for about a mile (1.6km), passing the entrance to Cotchet Farm on the left. Continue walking along Fernden Lane.

5 Make for a signposted bridleway on the left. After a few paces reach a National Trust sign. Keep left here and follow the sunken path as it climbs between trees, steeply in places. On the higher ground, follow the path as it winds between bracken and silver birch. Fork right past a seat which takes advantage of a magnificent view, part obscured by trees. Keep the view on your right and walk along the level to the curved stone seat at what is known as the Temple of the Winds.

6 Take the path running up behind the seat, very soon keeping right and right again. Keep ahead past a path running off sharp right and then a flight of steps, and veer left or right at the next signposted fork: both paths soon merge again.

7 Continue ahead and veer right at the next fork. Keep ahead at the next junction, now following part of the Sussex Border Path again and retracing your initial outward steps. Veer to the right at the fork, still following the long-distance trail, and head back down the road to the entrance to the car park.

WHAT TO SEE Black Down's plateau was once an extensive heath created by grazing and managed as common pasture with bracken cut and gathered for bedding. Thousands of years of grazing sustained our heathlands, but since 1950 nearly half of it has been lost. Before grazing stopped, much of the site consisted of gorse and heathland plant. Later, Scots pine, birch and rhododendron began to grow. The main summit area is dominated by heather and bell heather, with a variety of wetland plants including cross-leaved heath, round-leaved sundew and common and hare's tail cotton grasses. Pine woodland is prolific here, with rowan, birch, gorse, bramble and bilberry. Birds include nuthatch, woodcock, nightjar, linnet and yellowhammer.

WHILE YOU'RE THERE The views from the Temple of the Winds are outstanding. Tennyson's old summerhouse stood near the memorial seat here.

Fernhurst's Iron Industry

DISTANCE 6 miles (9.7km)   MINIMUM TIME 3hrs

ASCENT/GRADIENT 480ft (146m) ▲▲▲   LEVEL OF DIFFICULTY +++

PATHS Mixture of woodland and farmland

DOG FRIENDLINESS Near private houses, signs request dogs be on lead

SEE MAP AND INFORMATION PANEL FOR WALK 43

To extend Walk 44 to visit Fernhurst, once an important village at the centre of the Wealden iron industry, and perhaps have lunch at the Red Lion, turn right at the sign for Sheetlands at Point ❹. Follow the tarmac drive through the trees down to a bridleway sign.

Go left up the bank, veering right at the top, and keep to the path as it runs above the drive. Pass above houses and turn right, just after a thatched house, by a waymarker post. Descend an enclosed path, which bends left at the bottom and immediately right by a pond and climbs quite steeply.

Turn left at a signposted T-junction and then, ignoring a track to the left, follow the driveway past an ornate lamp standard. Turn left on a signposted path, along a line of trees and over stiles. Cross over a driveway and take the path opposite, heading towards Fernhurst. Join a tarmac drive, turn left at the road and then walk through the village to the Red Lion, overlooking the spacious green.

On leaving the inn, turn immediately left and follow the tarmac drive, which soon becomes an unmade woodland track and later bears left then right over a stream. Turn left by a wooden barn and cottages and veer right at the next waymarked fork.

Now begin a moderate ascent through the trees. Cross a wide track and continue the climb up through the woodland. Keep right by a house called Reeth. The track bends round to the left and runs up to a junction with a minor road. Turn right, rejoin Walk 43 and follow Points ❺, ❻ and ❼ back to the car park.

WHERE TO EAT AND DRINK The Red Lion at Fernhurst occupies a lovely position overlooking the village green. On warm summer days, there's nothing to beat sitting outside this 500-year-old building and enjoying its picturesque setting. There's a good range of beers and a varied menu. Bar meals are served all week and the restaurant is open every day.

History on the Downland at East Lavant

DISTANCE 5 miles (8km)	MINIMUM TIME 2hrs

ASCENT/GRADIENT 550ft (168m) ▲▲▲   LEVEL OF DIFFICULTY ✦✦✦

PATHS Downland paths, bridleways and tracks. Includes a section of Goodwood Lavant Valley Cycle Route

LANDSCAPE Open downland and farmland

SUGGESTED MAP AA Walker's Map 20 Chichester & The South Downs

START/FINISH Grid reference: SU872110

DOG FRIENDLINESS Long stretches of track where dogs can run free. Keep under control on village roads and patches of farmland

PARKING Free parking at Seven Points, Goodwood Country Park (closes at dusk)

PUBLIC TOILETS None on route

On a fine day, the views from the car park alone at the start of this spectacular walk will lift your spirits. The coastal plain stretches out below you, with Chichester to the south, and beyond to the west the Isle of Wight clearly visible. But there's even better to come from the top of the nearby Trundle hill-fort, which affords an unforgettable view of the Sussex countryside.

AN ANCIENT HILL-FORT

The Trundle – from the Old English meaning circle – crowns the top of St Roche's Hill, the site, too, of two large radio masts. (Whatever they lack in aesthetic value, they do provide a useful landmark.) The Trundle, made up of a ditch, dyke and banks, stands 675ft (206m) above sea level and began life as a Neolithic enclosure. Iron Age people later occupied the site and during the Middle Ages, a chapel stood here. Later still, a windmill crowned the summit which was adorned with eight masts during World War II.

On the far side of this impressive fortified hilltop, Goodwood Racecourse suddenly looms into view, catching you completely by surprise when you walk up here. The gleaming grandstand and the racecourse's natural amphitheatre setting create a stunning picture. It's a good, free vantage point for viewing the races. It's well worth walking at least part way round the ramparts to enjoy the views to the full, splendid towards the south coast, but lovely inland too.

GOODWOOD

Goodwood House, one of the finest stately homes in the country, has been the home of the Dukes of Richmond and Lennox for over 300 years. Situated a couple of miles to the east of the walk, surrounded by mature parklands, it's open to visitors from March to October. As well as the racecourse, Goodwood also has a motor racing circuit – its Festival of Speed is a well-known annual event. The noise level is monitored and categorised, so if you're after peace and quiet it's worth checking the website calendar which shows the noise category for each day when events are taking place.

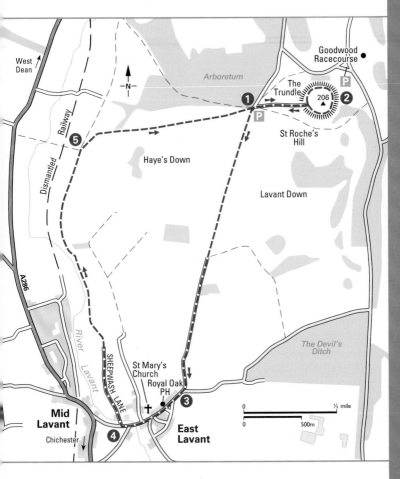

1 From the car park, make your way up the track towards the masts. Continue ahead at the top, then bear slightly right to the trig point and savour the views.

2 Drop down to the ramparts and walk round and back down to the car park. Turn left downhill on a stony track, heading south towards

Chichester and East Lavant. The views are glorious, the scene dominated by a vast patchwork of fields and hedgerows, and the distant spire of Chichester Cathedral acting as a useful directional landmark. On the way down you may also spot in the distance to the southwest Portsmouth's striking Spinnaker Tower. This track is part of a popular cycle route, so look out for cyclists who come beetling up behind you, leaving clouds of dust in their wake on a summer's day. Your walk may also be accompanied by the drone of light aircraft overhead as planes take off and land at nearby Goodwood aerodrome. In due course, trees, bushes and margins of underbrush obscure the fine views in places.

❸ After 1.5 miles (2.4km) reach the village of East Lavant, turn right, and walk along the main street. Pass the Royal Oak and the parish church and cross the bridge over the weed-choked River Lavant. Veer right just beyond it into Sheepwash Lane and pause for a moment or two to study the simple war memorial at the corner of the road. Farmers once washed their sheep in the river here – hence the name.

❹ Bear right over a brick bridge after 70yds (64m) at the sign for Staple House Farm to follow the bridleway. Pass the turning on the right to the farm and keep straight on. The track ahead can be flooded after periods of heavy rain, especially in winter. The bridleway divides into two parallel paths at one point, but your choice of route doesn't matter as they unite further on. Keep ahead, passing a left turn towards some waterworks. The path becomes enclosed by trees and scrub before reaching a gate. Pass through, and the surroundings are once again open and exposed, with the walk keeping to the right-hand side of the boundary fence. Continue to a gate and 25yds (23m) beyond it arrive at a fingerpost marking a junction of bridleways, ignoring another gate on the left.

❺ Veer half right at this point, following the outline of the path as it runs diagonally across the grassy slope. The path reaches a gate in the line of trees. Looking back, there are fine downland views stretching to Kingley Vale on the horizon, with the A286 threading its way across the landscape. Pass through the gate and follow the path between fields, the spire of Chichester Cathedral seen over to the right, reaching skyward. Wild poppies grow in the field-edges here, adding an extra dash of colour. A large house with sash windows and a slate roof looms into view ahead as you approach the end of the walk. Continue past the house back to the car park.

WHERE TO EAT AND DRINK The Royal Oak at East Lavant is ideally placed. Although more of a restaurant than a pub, it has a small bar and terrace and a full menu. Children and dogs are allowed inside. You might find an ice cream van at Seven Points.

WHAT TO SEE In summer, keep an eye out for chalk downland flowers such as harebells, scabious and orchids. Downland birds that may be spotted include skylarks, yellowhammers, buzzards and kestrels. The skylark is the bird that epitomises the Downs, with its distinctive high-pitched melodies. The males hover and sing at a considerable height, usually appearing to the naked eye as just a dot in the sky. The Downs are famous for their butterflies, so look out, too, for chalkhill blues, marbled whites and silver fritillaries.

WHILE YOU'RE THERE Have a look round East Lavant and visit the Church of St Mary's. The village lies on the River Lavant, a winter bourne which has been known to dry up for years at a time. The river, which rises near East Dean, passes through Chichester to reach Chichester Harbour.

Espying Chichester's Spire

DISTANCE 4.5 miles (7.2km)	MINIMUM TIME 2hrs

ASCENT/GRADIENT Negligible ▲▲▲   LEVEL OF DIFFICULTY ✚✚✚

PATHS Urban walkways, tow path and field paths

LANDSCAPE Mixture of city streets and open countryside

SUGGESTED MAP AA Walker's Map 20 Chichester & The South Downs

START/FINISH Grid reference: SU858044

DOG FRIENDLINESS On lead in Chichester and farmland. Off lead by canal

PARKING Fee-paying car park in Avenue de Chartres

PUBLIC TOILETS At car park and elsewhere in Chichester

A stroll through the quaint streets of Chichester is the only way to appreciate all that this small but very beautiful cathedral city has to offer. Chichester's origins date back as far as the late Iron Age, and it was settled by the Romans in about AD 200. They built the walls, which can still be clearly identified. During the Middle Ages the city witnessed the building of the great cathedral and its precincts. Later, in the boom years of the 18th century, Chichester really came into its own when wealthy merchants, engaged in the shipping industry and the corn trade, began to build many of the fine houses and civic buildings you see today.

HEART OF THE CITY

Chichester's cathedral, the Mother Church of the Diocese of Chichester, is the focal point of the city. The spire, a local landmark, collapsed in 1861 and was rebuilt under the supervision of Sir George Gilbert Scott, who was also responsible for St Pancras station and the Albert Memorial in London. Ranging from Norman to Perpendicular in style, this magnificent building includes the site of a shrine to St Richard, Bishop of Chichester in the 13th century, tapestries by John Piper and Romanesque stone carvings. Another memorable feature is Graham Sutherland's painting, which depicts Christ appearing to St Mary Magdalen on the first Easter morning.

From the cathedral the walk heads down West Street to the intricately decorated Market Cross, built at the beginning of the 16th century and considered to be one of the finest of its kind in the country. It was Bishop Story who made a gift of the cross to the city. He also endowed the Prebendal School in West Street. Situated at the hub of the Roman street plan and distinguished by its flying buttresses, the cross was built to provide shelter for traders who came to Chichester to sell their wares. Make your way up North Street to the Council House, built in 1731 and famous for its huge stone lion and Roman stone. The Latin inscription records the dedication of a Roman temple to Neptune and Minerva. From here it's an easy stroll south to the Pallants, a compact network of narrow streets and elegant houses.

Leaving the city, the walk then follows the Chichester section of the Portsmouth and Arundel Canal out into the countryside and south to the village of Hunston. Buildings change and cities continue to evolve, but Chichester's most famous landmark, the elegant spire of its cathedral, remains in view for part of this pleasant walk out and back along the canal.

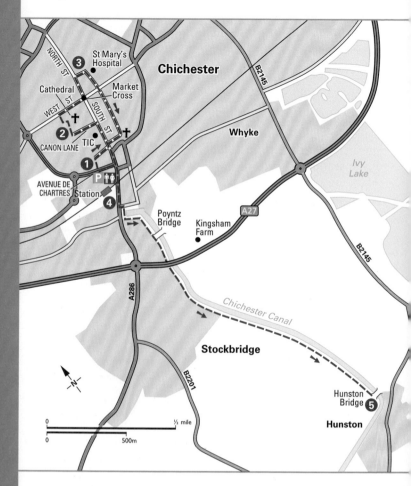

1 Leave the car park at the northeast corner (the other end from the entrance), cross the footbridge over the Avenue de Chartres and head towards Chichester city centre.

Turn right at the city map and then left into South Street. Bear left through an archway leading into Canon Lane, just beyond the tourist information centre. Turn right into

St Richard's Walk and approach the magnificent Chichester Cathedral.

❷ Swing left at the cloisters, then left again to keep the stone wall on your left. Make for the West Door and pass the Bell Tower to reach West Street. Bear right here. Across the road is a converted church, now a pub. The north face of Chichester Cathedral is clearly seen as you head along West Street. On reaching the Market Cross, turn left into North Street and bear right immediately beyond the historic many-arched, red brick Council House into Lion Street.

❸ Walk along to St Martin's Square and opposite you at this point is St Mary's Hospital. Turn right and pass the Hole in the Wall pub to reach East Street. Glance to the left and you can pick out the Corn Exchange. Go straight over into North Pallant and walk along to Pallant House Gallery, one of England's finest collections of modern art. Head straight on into South Pallant and follow the road round to the right, passing Christ Church on the left. Turn left at the next next junction and keep ahead at the following junction into Southgate.

❹ Cross the railway at Chichester station and then swing left to reach the canal basin. Follow the tow path around the right side of the basin to Poyntz Bridge, dated 1820, and continue to the next bridge, which carries the A27 Chichester bypass. Keep going as far as the next footbridge, Hunston Bridge (confusingly labelled Poyntz Bridge on OS maps, since this is where the latter was originally situated before being relocated).

❺ Admire the view from the bridge of the canal with the cathedral in the distance, the scene depicted in a painting by J M W Turner. Retrace your steps towards Chichester. Just after crossing the railway line, turn left then right to return to the start.

WHERE TO EAT AND DRINK There are dozens of restaurants, cafes and pubs from which to choose in Chichester, including the Cloisters Café at the cathedral and the acclaimed Field & Fork restaurant at the Pallant Gallery. The former prides itself on using fair trade suppliers and freshly cooked food, while the latter uses home-grown and locally sourced produce for its seasonal menus. Out of the city there's the Spotted Cow at Hunston.

WHAT TO SEE In addition to the remains of the Roman city walls, there is St Mary's Hospital of the Blessed Virgin Mary in St Martin's Square, founded between 1158 and 1170. Originally a hospital, it later became almshouses and is one of Chichester's most historic buildings. Visitors can make an appointment with the guide. In the nearby Pallants is Pallant House, built by Chichester wine merchant Henry Peckham in 1712. The house is Queen Anne style and each room reflects a particular period of its history.

WHILE YOU'RE THERE Enjoy a trip on the tree-lined Chichester Canal. It's part of the Portsmouth and Arundel Canal, built to link with other rivers and navigations to form an inland waterway between London and Portsmouth. Designed by John Rennie and opened in 1822, the canal acted as a through route until 1855 and the Chichester stretch was built to take ships.

Overleaf: Chichester Cathedral (Walk 47)

A Harbour Walk at West Itchenor

DISTANCE 3.5 miles (5.7km)	**MINIMUM TIME** 1hr 30min

ASCENT/GRADIENT Negligible ▲▲▲   **LEVEL OF DIFFICULTY** +++

PATHS Shoreline, field tracks and paths

LANDSCAPE Open farmland and coastal scenery

SUGGESTED MAP AA Walker's Map 20 Chichester & The South Downs

START/FINISH Grid reference: SU798012

DOG FRIENDLINESS Waterside paths are ideal for dogs but keep under control on stretches of open farmland and on short section of road. Dogs permitted on harbour water tour

PARKING Large pay-and-display car park in West Itchenor

PUBLIC TOILETS West Itchenor

Weekend sailors flock to Chichester's vast natural harbour, making it one of the most popular attractions on the south coast. The harbour has about 50 miles (81km) of shoreline and 17 miles (28km) of navigable channel, though there is almost no commercial traffic. The Romans cast an approving eye over this impressive stretch of water and established a military base and harbour at nearby Fishbourne after the Claudian invasion of Britain in AD 43. Charles II had a fondness for the area too and kept a yacht here.

Situated at the confluence of the Bosham and Chichester channels of the estuary is the small sailing village of Itchenor. Originally named Icenor, this picturesque settlement started life as a remote, sparsely populated community, but by the 18th century it had begun to play a vital role in the shipbuilding industry. Small warships were built here by the merchants of Chichester, though in later years shipbuilding ceased altogether and any trace of its previous prosperity disappeared beneath the houses and the harbour mud. However, the modern age of leisure and recreation has seen a revival in boat building and yachting, and today Itchenor is once again bustling with boat yards, sailors and chandlers.

IMPORTANT TIDAL HABITAT

But there is much more to Chichester Harbour than sailing. Take a stroll along the harbour edge and you will find there is much to capture the attention. With its intertidal habitats, the harbour is a haven for plant life and wildlife. Wading birds such as the curlew, redshank and dunlin can be seen using their differently shaped bills to extract food from the ecologically rich mudflats and terns may be spotted plunging to catch fish. Plants include sea lavender and glasswort, and many of them are able to resist flooding and changing saltiness. Salt marsh is one of the typical habitats of Chichester Harbour and the plants which make up the marsh grow in different places according to how often they are flooded.

Stand on the hard at West Itchenor and you can look across the water towards neighbouring Bosham, pronounced 'Bozzum'. Better still, take the ferry over there and explore the delights of this picturesque harbour village. It was from here that Harold left for Normandy before the Norman Conquest of 1066. 'The sea creek, the green field, the grey church,' wrote Tennyson and this sums up perfectly the charm of this unspoilt corner of Sussex. Take a little time to look at the Church of the Holy Trinity and its Saxon tower base while you're there.

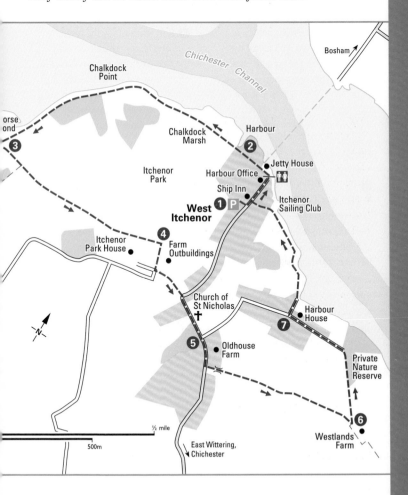

❶ From the car park walk along to the road and bear left, heading towards the harbour front. Pass the

Ship Inn and make your way down to the water's edge. Look for the harbour office and the toilets and follow the footpath to the left of Jetty House.

2 Cut between hedging and fencing to reach a boat yard and then continue ahead on the clear surfaced path, passing a permissive path on the left that leads back to the car park. Keep left at the next junction and shortly the path breaks cover to run by the harbour and its expanses of mudflats. Cross Chalkdock Marsh and continue on the waterside path.

3 Keep going until you reach a footpath sign. Turn left here by a sturdy old oak tree and follow the path away from the harbour edge, keeping to the right-hand boundary of the field. Cross a stile to join a track on a bend and continue ahead, still maintaining the same direction. Pass Itchenor Park House on the right and approach some farm outbuildings.

4 Turn right by a brick-and-flint farm outbuilding and follow the path, soon merging with a concrete track. Walk ahead to reach the next junction and turn left by a white gate, down to the road. Keep ahead here and soon

reach the Church of St Nicholas, with Itchenor Village Pond just beyond.

5 Follow the road beyond Oldhouse Farm and then turn left at the footpath sign to cross a footbridge. Keep to the right of several barns and follow the path straight ahead across the field. Pass a line of trees and keep alongside a ditch on the right into the next field. The path follows the hedge line, making for the field corner. Ahead are the buildings of Westlands Farm.

6 Turn sharp left by the footpath sign and follow the path across the field. Skirt the woodland, part of a private nature reserve, and veer left at the entrance to the Spinney. Follow the residential drive to Harbour House.

7 Turn right just beyond it and follow the path along the edge of the harbour. Keep going along here until you reach Itchenor Sailing Club. Bear left and walk up the drive to the road. Opposite you should be the Ship Inn. Turn left to return to the car park.

WHERE TO EAT AND DRINK The Ship Inn at West Itchenor dates back to 1803 and was largely rebuilt after a fire in the 1930s. The spacious interior fills up on summer weekends, but there is a good choice of food.

WHAT TO SEE Just over halfway round the walk you pass the delightful 13th-century Church of St Nicholas, dedicated to the patron saint of children and seafarers. The little church, which has a lychgate, is usually open and inside there are some fascinating treasures. Changes in the window arrangements were made in the 14th century to provide additional light and there have been a number of alterations and additions over the years.

WHILE YOU'RE THERE Enjoy a water tour of Chichester Harbour during the summer months, or go in winter when there are regular trips for birding, accompanied by an expert guide. These tours enable you to appreciate the harbour's treasures first-hand and see at close quarters some of the many vessels that use it. There are about 12,000 resident boats, with many visiting yachts from the USA, the Far East and Europe.

Views at Kingley Vale

DISTANCE 5 miles (8km)   MINIMUM TIME 2hrs

ASCENT/GRADIENT 440ft (134m) ▲▲▲   LEVEL OF DIFFICULTY +++

PATHS Mostly woodland paths and downland tracks

LANDSCAPE Dense woodland and rolling downland

SUGGESTED MAP AA Walker's Map 20 Chichester & The South Downs

START/FINISH Grid reference: SU815126

DOG FRIENDLINESS Under control in Stoughton village. Elsewhere off lead
unless signs state otherwise

PARKING Free car park at Stoughton Down

PUBLIC TOILETS None on route

You might not expect to find the largest yew forest in Europe tucked
away in the South Downs, but that's exactly where it is. This remote
downland landscape, covering more than 200 acres (81ha) is cloaked
with 30,000 yew trees. Once a wartime artillery range, Kingley Vale
became one of Britain's first nature reserves in 1952. Today, it is
managed by Natural England.

GNARLED AND TWISTED TRUNKS

Silent, isolated and thankfully inaccessible by car, the grove of ancient
yew trees at Kingley Vale is a haven for ramblers and naturalists. The
walk skirts the forest but if you have the time to explore, the effort is
certainly worthwhile.

   The yew is one of our finest trees and can live up to 2,000 years.
It is usually a large but squat tree, its branches and dark green needles
conspiring to create a dense evergreen canopy which allows little light
to filter through to the forest floor. With their deep red trunks, branches
and shallow roots twisted into monstrous shapes and gargoyle faces,
some of the yews at Kingley Vale are thought to be over 500 years old.

   Even on the sunniest day, the scene amid the tangle of boughs is
eerily dark, strange and mystical, like something from the pages of a
children's fairy tale. The yew has always featured strongly in folklore
and, according to legend, this place was a meeting point for witches
who engaged in pagan rites and wove magical spells here. Danes and
Druids are also believed to haunt the vale.

ANCIENT ORIGINS

Various theories about the origin of the forest have been suggested but
it is thought that the site marks the spot where a 9th-century battle
against the Vikings took place. Some sources suggest the trees were
planted here to guide pilgrims travelling across the South Downs to

Canterbury. Long before the yews began to grow, Bronze Age kings were buried here, confirmed by various tumuli on the Ordnance Survey map.

The trees may be the dominant feature at Kingley Vale but the grove is teeming with wildlife. The delightful green woodpecker, noted for its distinctive colouring, inhabits the reserve, one of 57 species of breeding bird found here. The bee orchid blooms in June while mountain sheep and wild fallow deer keep the turf short for 200 other species of flower. If you're lucky, you might spot a fox or a kestrel.

Beginning just outside the village of Stoughton, the walk immediately makes for dense woodland before climbing quite steeply to the spectacular viewpoint overlooking Kingley Vale. The reserve, renowned for its ecological importance, covers the southern chalk slopes of 655ft (206m) high Bow Hill and from this high ground the views are tremendous.

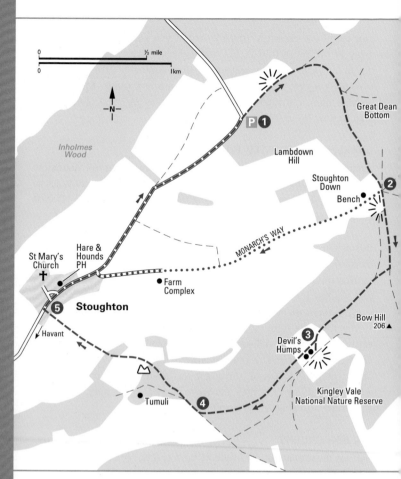

① Take the bridleway (signposted from the car park entrance), leading away from the road and through a metal barrier, skirting dense woodland. There are striking views on the left over pastoral, well-wooded countryside. Keep right at a fork and follow the stony path as it curves to the right. Veer slightly right as signposted at the next waymarked fork and begin a gradual ascent beneath the boughs of beech and oak trees.

② Eventually break cover from the trees at a major junction of waymarked tracks. Go straight on, looking to the right for spectacular views. After 125yds (41m), fork left at the next bridleway sign and join a path running parallel to the track. Cut between trees and keep going for 0.25 miles (400m) until you reach a waymarker post. Fork right here. Keep to the waymarked path as it runs down the slope. Rejoin the stony track, turning left to follow it up the slope towards Bow Hill.

③ On reaching the Devil's Humps, veer off the path by a sign for Kingley Vale National Nature Reserve to enjoy the magnificent vistas across the downland countryside. The view to the north, over remote woodland and downland, is impressive enough, but the panorama to the south is particularly outstanding. Immediately below you are the trees of Kingley Vale. Return to the nature reserve sign and continue the previous direction along the track, keeping to the right of the Devil's Hump and re-entering the forest.

④ Bear right at the next main junction and follow the bridle track alongside a field. On the left are glimpses of Chichester Harbour, with its complex network of watery channels and sprawling mudflats, and the Isle of Wight beyond. Soon enter the trees and ignore a left fork; near here are more ancient burial tumuli. Follow the track down through the woodland and out into the open, Stoughton in view below. Turn right at the road.

⑤ Pass the entrance to St Mary's Church on the left, followed by the Hare & Hounds pub. Continue through the village and on the right is the Monarch's Way. Follow the road out of Stoughton back to the car park.

WHERE TO EAT AND DRINK Have a picnic by the Devil's Humps or stop off towards the end of the walk at the Hare & Hounds in Stoughton. This striking flint building dates back to around the 17th century and was originally built as two cottages. Choose from a good snack menu, which includes sandwiches and baguettes, or go for something more exciting such as roast beef salad, lasagne or steak. Everything is cooked on the premises and there are various game dishes in season. There is a terrace in front, and children and dogs are welcome.

WHILE YOU'RE THERE Visit Stoughton's 11th-century cruciform church of St Mary. The exterior is barn-like, bulky even, and inside it is unexpectedly spacious. The south transept was converted into a tower in the 14th century, the nave is over 30ft (9m) high and there is a striking Norman arch with a triple layer of roll mouldings.

Stoughton and the Monarch's Way

DISTANCE 3.5 miles (5.7km)   MINIMUM TIME 1hr 30min

ASCENT/GRADIENT 334ft (102m) ▲▲▲   LEVEL OF DIFFICULTY ✚✚✚

SEE MAP AND INFORMATION PANEL FOR WALK 48

If you don't want to make the climb up to Kingley Vale, or haven't got the time, you can take a short cut to Stoughton, following the route of the Monarch's Way, a 615-mile (984km) trail following the escape route of Charles II after the Battle of Worcester in 1651. Though a little less dramatic than the main Walk 48, this shorter alternative still captures the essence of the beautiful wooded South Downs country.

Follow the instructions for Walk 48 from the car park at Stoughton Down as far as the major junction at Point ❷. Turn right here and follow the long-distance trail over Stoughton Down, down towards the village. On the right-hand side, just along here, is a nicely placed wooden bench seat.

Follow the bridleway until it branches off to the right and go straight ahead on the waymarked public footpath. Follow the unsurfaced farm road to some substantial outbuildings for cattle, then continue along to the farm complex proper. On reaching the surfaced road, turn right and go directly back to the car park. Alternatively, if time allows, bear left here and walk along to the 11th-century church.

WHAT TO LOOK OUT FOR Various Bronze Age barrows (burial mounds), known as the Devil's Humps, can be seen up on Bow Hill. There are several legends on the South Downs concerning the Devil. This one suggests that anyone who runs round the humps six times will experience a sighting! As you approach the village of Stoughton on the main walk, look for a memorial stone to the right of the path. It was here in this field, in November 1940, that a Polish pilot officer, based at nearby RAF Tangmere, died when his Hurricane crashed following aerial combat with a German ME109. The memorial is sometimes strewn with poppies and other flowers.

Wide Horizons at West Wittering

DISTANCE 5 miles (8km)	MINIMUM TIME 2hr 30min

ASCENT/GRADIENT Negligible ▲▲▲   LEVEL OF DIFFICULTY ✦✦✦

PATHS Beach and water-side paths, road and private drives

LANDSCAPE Wide views, natural tidal inlet

SUGGESTED MAP AA Walker's Map 20 Chichester & The South Downs

START/FINISH Grid reference: SZ772978

DOG FRIENDLINESS Off lead on harbour-side paths. On lead in West Wittering. Dogs excluded from main swimming beach from May to September. Keep under control on East Head

PARKING Large fee-paying car park at West Wittering beach

PUBLIC TOILETS West Wittering beach and village

The seaside community of West Wittering is tucked away from the rest of Sussex on a peninsula at the mouth of Chichester Harbour. Despite the hordes of summer visitors who flock to the beach, it retains a dignified air of how small seaside towns used to be. The village evolved mainly during the first half of the 20th century, though some elderly residents recall this stretch of coast before it became fashionable – when open fields extended to the superb beach, providing a natural playground for children.

EAST HEAD

This slender spit of sand and shingle dunes at the mouth of Chichester Harbour has changed dramatically during the last two centuries, influenced by the elements. In 1786 the spit pointed across the entrance of the harbour towards Hayling Island, but since then its position has moved and it now points north. In November 1963 part of East Head was breached by high spring tides and its future looked uncertain. The following year the dunes were artificially reshaped and stabilised before being handed to the National Trust in 1966. Work to restore this sensitive natural feature of the Sussex coast has continued ever since. Visitors are requested to use the boardwalks to avoid trampling the marram grass – which is essential for helping stabilise the sand – and to stay out of the fenced- or roped-off areas. The walk is most enjoyable at low tide when large expanses of sand are revealed.

WILDLIFE

Between East Head and the mainland is an area of salt marsh known as Snowhill Creek, which provides a feeding ground for thousands of birds. Among the large numbers of wintering waders and wildfowl found here are Brent geese, shelduck, redshank and curlew. Up to 45,000 Brent geese fly into Chichester Harbour from September to December. Of that number around 5,000 settle at Snowhill Creek and graze the fields of West Wittering Estate. Out on the shingle banks of East Head, ringed plovers nest. Their eggs are beautifully camouflaged to look like pebbles. Common and grey seals are both found in Chichester Harbour. When the tide is out you may spot them basking on mud banks.

The West Wittering Estate company was formed in 1952 by local residents who clubbed together to buy the land to prevent it from being developed as a holiday complex and to preserve it for public enjoyment. The beach can be very crowded on sunny summer weekends.

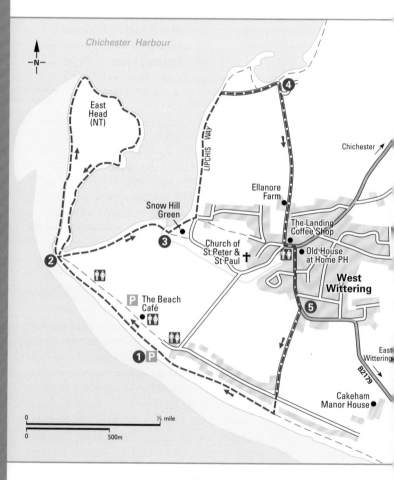

1 Follow the drive through the extensive car park, and join the parallel shore path at the earliest opportunity. Pass a row of charming beach huts and a toilet block on the right. Continue ahead towards the mouth of Chichester Harbour, with Hayling Island seen on the far side. Make for the East Head National Trust information board.

2 Follow the beach round the sand dune spit (if you do go onto the dunes use the boardwalks). After completing the circuit, bear left along the path beside Chichester Harbour and look to the right for a glimpse of the tower at Cakeham Manor. A new flood defence has been built along here, the path running along the top of the embankment. Continue to the grassy open space of Snowhill Green, keeping along the left-hand side. Snow Hill, the part of West Wittering between the church and Chichester Harbour, has been suggested as the original Roman landing site in Britain.

3 Pass a footpath on the right and carry on along the harbour edge. Leaving West Wittering behind, the scrub-bordered path heads north, with open farmland on the right and the harbour and marsh landscape on the left. Eventually it bends right by a bird hide and seat. Continue along the tree-shaded footpath.

4 Turn right at the next footpath sign by a gate. Walk along Ellanore Lane, passing Ellanore Farm. On reaching the road, opposite the public conveniences, turn right if you want to visit the church. To continue on the main route, turn left to reach a junction and then bear right to walk through West Wittering. Pass the Old House at Home pub and further along the road continue past Seaward Drive on the left, a private estate.

5 As the road bends left, cross to the right and take Berry Barn Lane, along which runs a bridleway. Follow the lane and again the tower at Cakeham Manor can be seen just across the fields. On reaching the signs for East Strand and West Strand, go straight on to follow a path between panel fencing and bushes. With the beach ahead, turn right towards East Head and follow the path over the greensward. On the right is a row of striking villas. The path continues over sand dunes. Beyond the villas, swing right through one of several gaps along the hedge to return to the car park.

WHERE TO EAT AND DRINK The Beach Café at West Wittering beach has a coffee shop and take-away and there are also several outlets selling ice cream and drinks. In the village itself try The Landing coffee shop, which serves a selection of coffees and cakes as well as light lunches. Nearby is the Old House at Home, which offers a varied home-made menu that changes regularly.

WHAT TO SEE Cakeham Manor, originally a grand palace belonging to the Bishops of Chichester, lies close to the route of the walk, between West Wittering and neighbouring East Wittering. Its most prominent feature is the tall, distinctive tower which was added to the house in the 16th century and can be clearly seen rising above this flat landscape. The rest of Cakeham Manor dates from around 1800. Neither the house nor the tower is open to the public.

WHILE YOU'RE THERE Visit the church of St Peter and St Paul in West Wittering. Dating to the 12th century, it's a lovely peaceful place to call in at, especially after a windswept walk round East Head. It is, in fact, the third or fourth church on this site, the earliest built around AD 770, shortly after St Wilfrid started converting the South Saxons (from whom Sussex takes its name) to Christianity.

Titles in the Series